Prepare for the Great Tribulation and the Era of Peace

Prepare for the Great Tribulation and the Era of Peace

Volume XXXVIII:
Jan. 1, 2005 – Mar. 31, 2005

by John Leary

PUBLISHING COMPANY
P.O. Box 220 • Goleta, CA 93116
(800) 647-9882 • (805) 692-0043 • Fax: (805) 967-5133
www.queenship.org

Dedication

To the Most Holy Trinity

God

The Father, Son and Holy Spirit

The Source of

All

Life, Love and Wisdom

Cover art by Josyp Terelya

© 2005 Queenship Publishing - All Rights Reserved.

Library of Congress Number # 95-73237

Published by:
  Queenship Publishing
  P.O. Box 220
  Goleta, CA 93116
  (800) 647-9882 • (805) 692-0043 • Fax: (805) 967-5133
  www.queenship.org

Printed in the United States of America

ISBN: 1-57918-276-3

Acknowledgments

It is in a spirit of deep gratitude that I would like to acknowledge first the Holy Trinity: Father, Jesus, and the Holy Spirit; the Blessed Virgin Mary and the many saints and angels who have made this book possible.

My wife, Carol, has been an invaluable partner. Her complete support of faith and prayers has allowed us to work as a team. This was especially true in the many hours of indexing and proofing of the manuscript. All of our family have been a source of care and support.

I am greatly indebted to Josyp Terelya for his very gracious offer to provide the art work for this publication. He has spent three months of work and prayer to provide us with a selection of many original pictures. He wanted very much to enhance the visions and messages with these beautiful and provocative works. You will experience some of them throughout these volumes.

A very special thank you goes to my spiritual director, Fr. Leo J. Klem, C.S.B. No matter what hour I called him, he was always there with his confident wisdom, guidance and discernment. His love, humility, deep faith and trust are a true inspiration.

Equal gratitude also goes to our new spiritual advisor, Father Donald McCarthy, C.S.B.

My appreciation also goes to Father John V. Rosse, my good pastor who is retiring from Holy Name of Jesus Church. He has been open, loving and supportive from the very beginning.

There are many friends and relatives whose interest, love and prayerful support have been a real gift from God. Our own Wednesday, Monday and First Saturday prayer groups deserve a special thank you for their loyalty and faithfulness.

Finally, I would like to thank Bob and Claire Schaefer of Queenship Publishing for providing the opportunity to bring this message of preparation, love and warnings to you, the people of God.

John Leary, Jr.

Declaration

The decree of the Congregation for the Propagation of the Faith, A.A.S.58, 1186 (approved by Pope Paul VI on October 14, 1966), states that the Nihil Obstat and Imprimatur are no longer required on publications that deal with private revelations, provided they contain nothing contrary to faith and morals.

The author wishes to manifest unconditional submission to the final and official judgement of the Magisterium of the Church.

His Holiness, Pope Urban VII states:
"In cases which concern private revelations, it is better to believe than to not believe, for if you believe, and it is proven true, you will be happy that you have believed, because our Holy Mother asked it. If you believe, and it should be proven false, you will receive all blessings as if it had been true, because you believed it to be true." (Pope Urban III, 1623-44)

The Catechism of the Catholic Church states:
Pg. 23, #67: "Throughout the ages, there have been so-called 'private revelations,' some of which have been recognized by the authority of the Church. They do not belong, however, to the deposit of faith. It is not their role to improve or complete Christ's definitive Revelation, but to help live more fully by it in a certain period of history. Guided by the Magisterium of the Church, the sensus fidelium knows how to discern and welcome in these revelations whatever constitutes an authentic call of Christ or His saints to the Church."

Publisher's Foreword

John has, with some exceptions, reported receiving messages twice a day since they began in July, 1993. The first of the day usually takes place during morning Mass, immediately after he receives the Eucharist. If the name of the church is not mentioned, it is a local Rochester, NY church. When out of town, the church name is included in the text. The second occurs in the evening, either at Perpetual Adoration or at the prayer group that is held at Holy Name of Jesus Church.

Various names appear in the text. Most of the time, the names appear only once or twice. Their identity is not important to the message and their reason for being in the text is evident. First names have been used, when requested by the individual.

We are grateful to Josyp Terelya for the cover art, as well as for the art throughout the book. Josyp is a well-known visionary and also the author of *Witness* and most recently *In the Kingdom of the Spirit*.

Early in 1999 John's bishop established a special commission to read John's published works and to talk to him about his religious experiences. The commission rendered its report in June. By letter of June 25, 1999 John was advised to have an explanatory note printed in the front of each book. This note appears on page xi of this edition.

Presently, the messages are being reviewed by Rev. Donald McCarthy, C.S.B., John's spiritual advisor.

This first edition under these rules has resulted in a delay of 90 days.

Late in October, 1999 John Leary and Carol were called to the office of the Diocese of Rochester for a meeting with the Vicar General. The result of the meeting was that they (the Diocese) are now allowing John to publish under their obedience. John was cautioned against mentioning the subjects called to John's attention in the bishop's original declaration (see page xi). John was further ordered to have his spiritual advisor read and approve each book. This is being done on each book.

This volume covers messages from Jan. 1, 2005 through Mar. 31, 2005. The volumes have been coming out quarterly due to the urgency of the messages.

Volume I: July, 1993 through June, 1994.
Volume II: July, 1994 through June, 1995.
Volume III: July, 1995 through July 10, 1996.
Volume IV: July 11, 1996 through September 30, 1996.
Volume V: October 1, 1996 through December 31, 1996.
Volume VI: January 1, 1997 through March 31, 1997.
Volume VII: April 1, 1997 through June 30, 1997.
Volume VIII: July 1, 1997 through September 30, 1997.
Volume IX: October 1, 1997 through December 31, 1997.
Volume X: January 1, 1998 through March 31, 1998.
Volume XI: April 1, 1998 through June 30, 1998.
Volume XII: July 1, 1998 through September 30, 1998.
Volume XIII: October 1, 1998 through December 31, 1998.
Volume XIV: January 1, 1999 through March 31, 1999.
Volume XV: April 1, 1999 through June 13, 1999.
Volume XVI: July 1, 1999 through September 30, 1999.
Volume XVII: October 1, 1999 through December 31, 1999.
Volume XVIII: January 1, 2000 through March 31, 2000.
Volume XIX: April 1, 2000 through June 30, 2000.
Volume XX: July 1, 2000 through September 30, 2000.
Volume XXI: October 1, 2000 through December 31, 2000.
Volume XXII: January 1, 2001 through March 31, 2001
Volume XXIII April 1, 2001 through June 30, 2001
Volume XXIV July 1, 2001 through Sept 30, 2001
Volume XXV October 1, 2001 through December 31, 2001
Volume XXVI January, 2002 through March 31, 2002
Volume XXVII April 1, 2002 through June 30, 2002
Volume XXVIII July 1, 2002 through September 30, 2002
Volume XXIX October 1, 2002 through December 31, 2002
Volume XXX January 1, 2003 through March 31, 2003
Volume XXXI April 1, 2003 through June 30, 2003.
Volume XXXII July 1, 2003 through September 30, 2003
Volume XXXIII October 1, 2003 through December 31, 2003
Volume XXXIV January 1, 2004 through March 31, 2004
Volume XXXV April 1, 2004 through June 30, 2004.
Volume XXXVI July 1, 2004 through September 30, 2004
Volume XXXVII October 1, 2004 through December 31, 2004
Volume XXXVIII January 1, 2005 through March 31, 2005

The Publisher

Readers Please Note:

Bishop Matthew H. Clark, Bishop of Rochester, has accepted the unanimous judgment of a special mixed Commission set up to study the writings of John Leary. After reading the volumes and meeting with Mr. Leary, they testified that they found him psychologically sound and spiritually serious. They concluded that his locutions are not a fraud perpetrated on the Catholic community. Nevertheless, in their judgment, his locutions are of human origin, the normal workings of the mind in the process of mental prayer.

Of grave concern to the Bishop and the Commission, however, are the errors that have found their way into his writings, two of which are most serious. The first is called by the Church "millenarianism." This erroneous teaching, contained in the first 6 volumes of *Prepare for the Great Tribulation and the Era of Peace,* holds that Christ will return to reign on the earth for a thousand years at the end of time. As the *Catechism of the Catholic Church* expresses it:

> The Antichrist's deception already begins to take shape in the world every time the claim is made to realize within history that messianic hope which can only be realized beyond history through the eschatological judgment. The Church has rejected even modified forms of this falsification of the kingdom to come under the name millenarianism ..." (CCC #676).

The second error is "anti-papalism." While the Church holds that the Pope "by reason of his office as Vicar of Christ, namely, as pastor of the entire Church, has full, supreme and universal power over the whole Church" (Vatican II, Constitution on the Church, #22), Mr. Leary's locutions select Pope John Paul II to be obeyed but his successor to be ignored as an "imposter pope." This erroneous teaching is found in all the volumes.

Because Mr. Leary has reaffirmed the teaching and discipline of the Church and acknowledged the teaching authority of John Paul II and Bishop Matthew H. Clark and their successors, Bishop Clark has permitted these volumes to be published with this warning to its readers appended.

Visions and Messages of John Leary:

Saturday, January 1, 2005: (Solemnity of Mary)
At St. John the Evangelist after Communion I could see a deep split in a large rock formation and there was water at the bottom and a ledge of protection at the bottom also. Jesus said: *"My people, this large split in the rock represents the many divisions among peoples that are causing your wars to continue. My peace on earth is what I bring to you on Christmas for your New Year. My blessings are always available for your peace makers and to settle your differences with one another. But there are those, who do not want to forget the wrongs done to them, and they continue to hold grudges or animosity to others. If you do not try to make peace, then you will condemn yourselves to constant wars. Wars never solve problems, but they cause more deaths and destruction. Wars promote hate instead of love and create deficits on both sides. At times disasters make men stop their wars and they struggle for survival. When you see the breadth of this latest devastation from the tidal waves, you see how small man is amidst the power of natural disasters. Life is too short to be killing each other before it is time, so make peace with each other instead of making war."*

Later, at St. Theodore's tabernacle I could see some insurgents carrying rocket propelled grenades and some small rockets. Jesus said: *"My people, year after year America has involved itself in many wars. Yet the results do not gain you anything and your war in Iraq has only caused a dragged out guerrilla war. You are spending billions of dollars and human lives in trying to establish a democracy that will be difficult to bring about in an Arab country. The only ones profiting from these wars are the arms dealers. Work to make peace and refuse to be misled by those trying to force wars on you that are not necessary. Love and compromise has more hope than fighting and hatred. Follow My call for peace and bring your troops home. After you leave Iraq, another militant will takeover despite your desires for a government to your liking. Then all of your troops' lives and the money spent will be in vain. If you spent the money for arms in helping the poor from the tidal wave, it would do more good than any of your killing."

Sunday, January 2, 2005: (Epiphany)
At Holy Name after Communion I could see Jesus on top of a large hill and people were struggling up the hill to get to their King. Jesus said: *"My people, even as the three kings came a long distance to give Me homage, you can come to give Me homage and reverence as well. Your struggle in life is made much less burdensome when you call on Me to help you through your trials. Looking up the mountain toward your goal in Me is how you keep focused on Me as your eternal destination. I also had to climb a hill to get to Calvary where I suffered and died for all of you. You can pick up your daily cross on your climb through life. By your love for Me and others in your prayers and good deeds, you can receive your reward and be resurrected later as I was. You can come to Me in Holy Communion at Mass or visit Me in Adoration or My tabernacle. Trust in Me and I will guard you from the evil one and provide for your every need."*

Monday, January 3, 2005: (Holy Name of Jesus)
At Holy Name after Communion I could see an Aurora Borealis in the sky at first and then it became a dawn with a large beautiful rainbow across the sky. Jesus said: *"My people, you are starting out fresh on a new year, and now is the time to think how you could change your life for the better. This beautiful rainbow is a ray of hope to show you how you can truly improve your life. Call on My help and I will inspire you with more love than grumbling and complaining. You need to smile with a happier disposition in order to spread love to those around you. Think on the bright side of how things could be instead of worrying that things*

could go wrong. *The more you spread love and cheer to oth the less sadness and hate there will be. Peace on earth and go will for all of mankind starts with each individual. Changing your life's outlook will put more joy in your life as you serve Me and your neighbor out of love. Reach out from your complacency and share your time and wealth with others, and your reward will be treasure in heaven. My Christmas Season is an uplifting celebration of life amidst the dullness of the winter blues. The Light of My grace will counter the fewer hours of daylight. Lift up your hearts with love of Me, and your life will be less burdensome."*

Later, at Our Lady of Lourdes Adoration I could see sharks in the water attacking unsuspecting victims. Jesus said: *"My people, these sharks in the water represent demons who are attacking unsuspecting sinners with their deadly temptations. When the devils urge you into mortal sin, it can be like death to the soul. The more you give into sin, the harder it will be to break sinful habits. You need My grace to come to Confession and cleanse yourself of deadly mortal sin. When you are starting another year, think of how you can please Me more with a better prayer life and a firm purpose to avoid your habitual sins. Breaking sinful habits means you need to avoid near occasions of sin, and have a will to fight off temptations. Do not be idle with your time or waste time on things that will not bring you closer to heaven. By focusing on Me in helping your neighbor, you can strive to imitate My life of love. Trust in Me that I can help you through all of life's trials, and you will be on the right path to heaven."*

Tuesday, January 4, 2005:

At Holy Name after Communion I could see two wedding rings under water and there was a churning of the water. Jesus said: *"My people, these two wedding rings are a sign of how I love all of My creations. Some wonder why I would allow so much death and destruction in this latest tidal wave and earthquake. This happened in the natural order of the plates coming together. More and more people are living in these coastal areas with very little warning of earthquakes. You saw similar destruction on the is-*

lands of the Carribean that were struck by the hurricanes. These areas are vulnerable to such natural disasters. Some nations have faced chastisements for their sins by natural disasters. Even America has been tested by hurricanes, tornadoes, and fire. You are being chastised for your abortions by your own natural disasters. Even with testing by these events, there is an opportunity for people in other areas to offer prayers and financial help to the needy. If you love Me, you will help your neighbors get back on their feet."

Later, at St. Theodore's Adoration I could see a red seaplane take off from the water and it flew up high to take an overall view of the destruction from the tsunami and the earthquake. Jesus said: *"My people, the more you view pictures of the destruction in several countries from the tidal wave, the more you can understand the scope of this disaster. This 9.0 earthquake had considerable force to send out these sixty foot tidal waves. The numbers of deaths and displaced people is climbing with each new report. One of the lessons that you can learn from this disaster is how insignificant man is compared to the fury of nature. No matter how many contributions that you make to society, they are still small compared to all of the people in the world. You may be small, but I love each one of you as precious to Me, and I care about your life and your soul. I died for the salvation of every soul from their sins. I do not want to lose even one soul, but each of you has free will to love Me or reject Me. When you choose Me or the world, there are consequences for your choices. Choosing to love Me could lead you to heaven, while choosing the world could lead you to eternal fire in hell. This is your soul's choice for eternity throughout your life here on earth by your daily choices."*

Wednesday, January 5, 2005:
At Holy Name after Communion I could see the facade of an old church that represented the Roman Catholic traditions to stand by. Jesus said: *"My people, the readings today speak about the contrast between love of God and fear. Those, who truly follow My Will in their lives and are united to Me in My Eucharist, have nothing to fear because I will take care of them for trusting in*

Me. On the other hand, there are those who refuse to accept Me and do not see themselves as sinners in need of forgiveness. While I still love these souls also, they are on the broad road to hell unless they change their ways. It is for this reason that I have sent My prophets, as yourself, to go out and preach repentance to all the nations. There are many who believe in Me, but they are

lukewarm and some have fallen away from their prayer traditions. Remember when I said to those who cried out only in calling 'Lord, Lord' that they give Me only lip service while their hearts are far from Me. There are some who will come to Me out of fear of punishment in hell for their sins, but the most desired way should be to come to Me out of love of your own free will. My mercy reaches out to all sinners, and you know that I will always forgive you if you come to Me with contrition for your sins. It is the souls who sin against the Holy Spirit with an unforgiving heart that cannot be forgiven. Unless you come forward and seek My forgiveness and are sorry for your sins, you cannot be saved. If you die in your sins without asking My forgiveness, you do risk the fires of hell. I am merciful, but I am just as well. That is why it is important for My evangelists to wake the people up spiritually because they must repent or be lost forever in hell. Many are reaching out to the victims of this latest disaster to save their physical lives. It is even more important to reach out to sinners to save their spiritual lives. There are two eternal destinations for souls in either heaven or hell, and you have only a short testing time on earth to choose between them. Those, who come to Me out of love or fear of hell, will be saved in heaven, but those, who refuse My love and reject Me in favor of worldly comforts and pleasures, are choosing hell and will be lost forever. You have until your dying breath to repent, so choose your destination wisely in every action of every day."*

Thursday, January 6, 2005:
At St. John the Evangelist after Communion I could see a large circling fan on the altar and it started spinning very fast until it appeared to be like a tornado drawing people's souls into the bright light in the middle. People's souls were being drawn to Jesus in the Warning experience. Jesus said: *"My people, a time is coming soon when your spirit bodies will all be drawn out of your bodies through a time tunnel to see Me as a bright light. You have seen previous messages describe this as the Warning, similar to those who have had near death experiences. Everyone in the world will experience this at the same time and I will reveal Myself to*

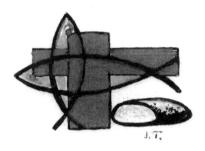

you as the Second Person of the Blessed Trinity. You will know beyond a doubt that this will be a supernatural experience. You will taste briefly the peace and joy of heaven to know what you are striving for. Then I will lead you through all of your life's experiences showing you your good and bad actions and how these influenced people as seen through their eyes. Then I will show you where you would go if you were to die that day at your judgment. Some will see purgatory, some will see hell, and very few will experience true heaven. You will see how your sins offended Me and have a great sense of guilt for your sins. You will be warned not to take the mark of the beast, nor worship the Antichrist. You will then return to your bodies as you are now and be given a second chance to reform your lives to love Me more and your neighbor. This Warning experience is a blessing of My mercy to wake everyone up from their spiritual complacency to deal with the most important choice in your life between Me in heaven or the devil in the world. Those, who choose to follow Me, will suffer much persecution, but your reward in heaven will far outweigh any of your worldly trials. Those, who choose worldly comforts and pleasures over Me, will face the actual hell on earth and in hell that they viewed in their Warning experience. This may be the last act of love for the lost souls to be saved. If they refuse Me, they will have to suffer the consequences of their actions."

Later, at the prayer group at Holy Name Adoration I could see the Blessed Mother holding the baby Infant Jesus in the stable. Jesus said: *"My people, you just celebrated My Blessed Mother's feast day of her Solemnity and the Epiphany of the three kings giving gifts to Me. Now after these devastating tidal waves, you are seeing many orphaned children and mothers looking for their lost children. Only instead of gifts at Christmas, many are sending financial gifts for food, water, and shelter for all the homeless. With millions without homes and food to eat, the compassion of the world is reaching out to help these less fortunate. What little these people had was taken away from them. All of you, who can well afford to donate to this cause, should send your alms to a reputable agency that will use the money for the most benefit. This is true giving out of love for seeing Me in these people."*

I could see some homes where people had taken down their Christmas trees. Jesus said: *"My people, this Christmas Season lasts just a short time and you relish My infancy but a moment. Some treasure My infancy throughout the whole year with either a Nativity Scene at your prayer altar, or a statue of My infancy. You can pray to their Infant King at any time and I will answer your prayers just the same as you pray to My adult images. So as you put away your Christmas decorations, think of Me throughout the whole year as the Light that comes into your dark world of sin."*

I could see many building structures that were damaged from these tidal waves. Jesus said: *"My people, you have seen much damage in Florida and the Carribean from the hurricanes. You suffered from oil and food shortages that resulted from these storms. America has wealth and resources to rebuild, but imagine the widespread destruction in Asia where they cannot afford to rebuild. Many are speaking of years to restore an economy back to normal in these poor islands. When you see people in need from storms, your heart goes out to want to help them. It is these donations that will help greatly and store treasure in heaven for the donors."*

I could see St. John the Baptist baptizing many in the Jordan. Jesus said: *"My people, with St. John's Baptism of Me you are bringing another Christmas Season to a close. There will be a month's time before you will start another Lenten Season. Almsgiving is one of the penances of Lent, but you already are donating to groups like Catholic Relief Services that are helping the victims of this terrible earthquake and tidal waves. You have some time to prepare what you will do for this coming Lent. This time of year is a chance to look at your spiritual life and how you can improve it in your striving for perfection. You need a consistent prayer life so you will keep your focus on Me. Many do extra prayers and daily Mass for Lent. Any way that you can show more love for Me and your neighbor will help your soul."*

I could see the feast days of many beautiful saints. Jesus said: *"My people, you have celebrated the Christmas Season and many beautiful saints' feast days that give you inspiration to be saints yourselves. The saints gave up much of this world's wealth to the poor and they wanted to depend entirely on My help and not any of their own. This is living in true trust of God even for what little you may have. The less you are influenced by wealth, possessions, and comforts, the easier it will be to detach yourself from earthly desires. It will be this severing of earth's ties that will make it easier also to aspire to be in heaven."*

I could see a large aisle through the middle of a church and then a representation of when Jesus was praised with palms as He came through Jerusalem. Jesus said: *"My people, it is easy to receive the food that I distributed to the 4,000 and the 5,000. It is also a blessing to have the dead raised to life and the sick healed back to good health. In the same way it is easier to be faithful to*

Me when everything is going well and you have all of your needs satisfied. But then when I brought My message of love, the people did not want to change their sinful pleasures, and they wanted to persecute Me. Again when you are persecuted for your faith, and your money trials test you, you grow weak in your suffering. Lift up your hearts and trust in Me to provide for you and I will take care of your needs. Give praise and glory to your God in good times and bad times."

I could see into far away hills and mountains as the Wise Men had to travel a great distance to see the newborn King. Jesus said: *"My people, even the Wise Men of the Epiphany are a good inspiration for you because you all have gifts that you can present to Me, not just at My crib, but you can share them with Me in the faces of the needy. You may be called to help and feed the poor in the physical life, or you may be called to spread My Gospel of love to save souls all over the world. Evangelization and healing gifts will help more spiritually give grace to souls through your talents and efforts. I love you always and I want you to share your faith in saving as many souls as you can."*

Friday, January 7, 2005:

At St. Charles after Communion I could see some fresh fallen snow that had a pure white appearance. Jesus said: *"My people, many times when it snows, people are more concerned with removing it from their driveways than looking at its own beauty. After all, snow is just frozen water, but it comes in a beauty of delicate snowflakes. If you looked closely at the structure of one snowflake, you could see the Creator's hand in its creation and the uniqueness of each flake. Without snow your winter landscape can be quite dull with no green vegetation. With a white covering there is a beauty in the purity of new fallen snow. You can liken snowflakes to the uniqueness of each person, and you can think of this pure white layer as a white purified soul with no sin after Confession. When snow is around for a while, it can pick up a darkness from dust and pollutants before it melts. This is like your souls after committing sin. But if you desire to have a white pure soul, you can go to frequent Confession and I will forgive you your sins, and restore your soul with grace to your former beauty at Baptism. Unfortunately, many are spiritually lazy and keep putting off Confession because they want to make more time for worldly activities than cleaning their soul's sins. You think dark or black covered snow looks so ugly, so imagine how unpleasant your sinful souls appear to Me. If you truly love Me, you will be sorry for your sins and try to make amends by asking My forgiveness in Confession. By keeping your soul pure, it will be easier to strive for being more perfect and your soul will always be prepared for your judgment when I take you home at death."*

Later, at St. Theodore's tabernacle I could see myself sitting on a chair inside a makeshift tent for a dwelling. Jesus said: *"My people, the people, who lost everything from the tidal wave in Indonesia, did not have much to begin with, so rebuilding will not be as difficult. Some may have to be satisfied with temporary dwellings as tents until their homes could be rebuilt. In America you have seen people lose their houses to tornadoes, hurricanes, and fires. You may have insurance to pay for rebuilding, but you would lose a lot more possessions if you lost your home than those in Asia. The more you have, the harder it would be to lose everything. Yet all that you have has been acquired, and you cannot take it with you beyond the grave. So do not let your possessions control you and run your life. When you are called to My refuges, you will have to leave most everything behind except your holy things and a few things for survival. So do not put a big importance on your possessions, but the spiritual things are of more importance. Love Me and your neighbor, and follow My Commandments. Then you will be focused on what will bring you to heaven."*

Saturday, January 8, 2005:

At St. John the Evangelist after Communion I could see some water and food supplies being packed off for the refugees from the tsunami. Jesus said: *"My people, no matter how strapped you think you may be for money, you cannot compare to the hungry, homeless survivors of this latest disaster in the Indian Ocean. So do not be personally stingy to these poor innocent victims. Every soul, no matter how poor, has the temple of the Holy Spirit residing in them. When you help them, you are helping Me in them. Many countries have responded and they will be rewarded. Just as you were moved to help the victims of last year's hurricanes, so you should equally be moved to help My little ones in Asia. Your reward will be stored in heaven for reparation due for your sins. I use your hands and legs to help those in need, so do not be lazy in fulfilling your Christian responsibility to help your neighbor."*

Sunday, January 9, 2005: (Baptism of Jesus)
At Holy Name after Communion I could see two beautiful trees in

the Garden of Eden. Jesus said: *"My people, when I created the Garden of Eden, the two trees in the vision are the Tree of Life and the Tree of the Knowledge of Good and Evil. (Gen. 2:9) It was the fruit of the Tree of the Knowledge of Good and Evil that I forbade Adam and Eve from eating or they would die. When they ate the fruit after being tempted by Satan, they committed original sin which everyone inherits at birth due to this fall. The consequences of original sin are death, sickness, weakness to sin, and banishment from the Garden of Eden. The gates of heaven were closed, but a Redeemer was promised by God. Today's reading about the Baptism of Myself displays the Blessed Trinity of the Three Persons including Myself, God the Father, and God the Holy Spirit. This Baptism represents Me as the new Adam in the Redeemer promised by God. I baptize with fire and My Baptism, that is available to everyone, will forgive your original sin and let you enter the faithful of My people. Baptism is your initiation into the faith and the beginning of your walk towards heaven where My death on the cross has opened the gates to enter. It is My Blood Sacrifice that also forgives all of your sins when you seek My forgiveness, so repent and be baptized."*

Later, at St. Cecilia's tabernacle I could see some old ornate churches and the people were following their traditions. Jesus said: *"My people, I am showing these traditional old churches, but it is how people lead their lives that matters most. You now have rampant divorce and living together without marriage. Your modern age has turned more evil because the people have lost their sense of shame in sin. In years past even getting a divorce was a stigma and parents would not allow their daughters to live with someone without marriage. You are too lax in not following My laws and each generation is further away from Me in sin. Because you are living in sin and not repenting of your sins, you are bringing My wrath on your country. You have laws favoring abortion and now protecting gay marriages. Pornography is all over your internet and your movies. You cannot flaunt your sins in front of Me and mock My laws, or you will face the chastisements that you are seeing in wars and natural disasters. If you want My blessings to return, then you must change your laws* and your lifestyles to following My laws. If you continue in your sins, then worse things will befall you."

Monday, January 10, 2005:
At Holy Name after Communion I could see a rush of water coming towards me. Jesus said: *"My people, many remember My promise to Noah that I would not destroy the world again with a flood and I gave you the rainbow as My covenant. Yet, I still use water in various forms as a chastisement for sin. You have seen the devastation of tidal waves that struck areas of pornography, prostitution, and trafficking of children for money. You have seen rainstorms, floods, and heavy snows in California where pornography and 'R' movies are made. Even snow came to Nevada that flaunts gambling and lewd dancing. When people's sins cry out for My justice, and you mock My laws, My wrath can be felt in various natural disasters in places of great sin. Do not think that you can defy Me without receiving some retribution. All over the world you are seeing chastisement for sin, but man is responsible because of his own sinful actions."*

Later, at St. Theodore's tabernacle I could see some medical wards where doctors were handling many cases at once because of the tidal waves. Jesus said: *"My people, the survivors of this disaster have had difficulty finding food and water, let alone medical help for injuries and diseases. Medical supplies and doctors are finally reaching the worst areas that were struck. Some remote areas are receiving more help than they ever received before this disaster. It is unfortunate that people sending donations have to be careful to give to reputable sources, or they could be tricked by thieves trying to steal their money. Giving alms to such a good cause, as helping people to survive, appears to have touched hearts to help the needy. Every soul that you help is like helping Me in that person. Once all of the major debris has been removed, then the people can try to have a more normal life. Give glory and thanks to God that you still have not yet been tested in such a disaster."*

Tuesday, January 11, 2005: (Anniversary of my son's death) At Holy Name after Communion I could see bright shooting rays of light coming from a beautiful rose. David (my son) said: *"My dear family, I am happy to greet you again with my love and I know how busy all of you are. I thank you for remembering me at every Holy Communion that you receive. I especially will be interceding with my prayers for the autistic boy, Noah, that you gave over to me to pray for. Whether you all are remembering me or not, you can express your care for me most by acknowledging your presence at my very grave site in the cemetery. This is real personal and shows Our Lord the beauty of my creation that you are giving glory to God for. I am in heaven, as you know, and I watch over each of you: Dad, Mom, Jeanette, Donna, and Catherine, as well as their own children. Do me this one favor of coming to my grave at least once a year."*

Later, at St. Theodore's Adoration I could see a house with snow blown all around it. Then I saw a blinding blizzard of snow. Jesus said: *"My people, you are seeing already how there is going to be more snow blizzards across your country than usual. California and some southern states have already had more snow than they have ever seen in the winter time. It is just a matter of time until the Northern and Eastern states will see more severe storms as well. The intensity of wind and blowing snow will be higher than ususal. This could cause considerably cold temperatures and more power outages. Your high fuel costs and the need for more fuel because of the cold will strain your monthly budgets. Much of the severe cold and intense wind is becoming worse due to the influence of microwave HAARP machines. The temperature extremes are becoming more influenced by your continuing pollution, and it is a sign of the hot and cold hearts of the lukewarm. In addition to preparing for your unusual weather, America needs to repent of its sins, and this coming Lent is another opportunity to change your lifestyles. You are too concerned with your possessions and comforts, but you will lose everything if you turn your back on Me. Increase your prayers and good deeds for Lent and you will be storing treasure in heaven."*

Wednesday, January 12, 2005:

At Holy Name after Communion I could see some clouds at night around a full moon and the clouds gradually covered the light of the moon making it darker. Jesus said: *"My people, the darkness of night represents the sin of your evil society. The clouds covering even the little light of the moon suggests that the evil of your actions is getting worse and more people are forgetting about Me in their lives. You claim to be a God-fearing people and you keep calling on Me to bless your country. But you are continuing your abortions, your sexual sins, and encouraging gay marriages. Instead of blessings, your actions are calling down My wrath in My chastisements. There are some prayer warriors among you and that has held back your total destruction, but most of your people give Me only lip service and their love for Me is weak, as they make their money and possessions their gods. Your moral life in America is like a sinking ship, and all of your physical things will be going down with you. Those, who will be going to My refuges, are like those escaping on lifeboats from this sinking ship that will be taken over by the one world people. You think that you are well off for many years to come, but I assure you only destruction and death lie in the future for those who disregard My laws and refuse to follow My Will. I keep calling America to wake up from its sin and put Me back into your laws and its lives."*

Later, at St. Theodore's Adoration I could see some green leafed trees against a blue sky. Then I saw the leaves turn brown from an insect infestation. Jesus said: *"My people, you are seeing more pestilence in the wake of serious natural disasters. In Africa and other areas locusts are devouring crops and anything green. Droughts and insect infestations can ruin your crops along with other disasters. This will worsen to cause a world famine with scarce food available for everyone. It is one thing to send surplus food to needy countries, or those suffering from the tidal waves. If food is scarce, then it will be hard to help people when everyone is starving. America with its vast food supplies of grain does not have near the amount of starving people as some third world countries do. The day that famine and drought strike America, it will be very difficult to believe because you have al-*

ways had plenty of food. When people start killing for food, you will see this as one of the signs to leave for your refuges. Trust in Me to feed you, even amidst the coming tribulation."

Thursday, January 13, 2005:
At St. John the Evangelist after Communion I could see an emergency telephone cord and then a long line of automated machines in a factory. Jesus said: *"My people, this vision is a wake up call to your people that your factory workers' days are numbered, and all manufacturing may cease to exist unless your government stops encouraging the export of your manufacturing jobs. You are reading in today's paper of the $60 billion of trade deficits and how your currency is down over 30 per cent to some currencies in the last few years. Your manufacturers by your current law are sending your jobs to foreign subsidiaries for low cost labor. The leaders and rich stockholders are profiting at the expense of lost manufacturing jobs of American workers. Your country as a whole is exporting its money, or lowering the value of your money at the same time. The American worker can see only low paying service jobs available with a lower standard of living for all but the rich. Unless your government changes its free trade to provide some protection for your workers, your government will not be able to collect enough taxes to survive, and all of your social security and medical payouts will not be able to be funded. Your trading partners are not playing on a fair basis because they are exploiting their people with slave wages. Even your illegal aliens are eroding your jobs and using your social service payouts. All of your financial woes and your natural disaster chastisements are wages of your sins in your greed for money and pleasures. Your moral and financial decay is pointing you toward the destruction of your country and the signs are all around you, but you do not want to believe it, or change your lifestyle of sin. You have seen other civilizations self-destruct for disobeying My laws. If you cannot learn from the history of your country, it will be repeated."*

Later, at the prayer group at Holy Name Adoration I could see a golden globe with rings around it that represented man's desire for golden riches and fame in awards. Jesus said: *"My people, every one of your souls its beautiful and special just because of who you are. You do not have to have riches to be famous in My eyes. You do not have to be a beauty queen or a renowned actor or actress to win your crown in heaven. All that I ask of you is to love Me and your neighbor as yourself. Imitate My life in following My Commandments and consecrate everything to My service. When you do everything for My sake, you do not desire earthly possessions, nor do you need anyone to tell you how important you are. Serving Me out of love and seeking My forgiveness of your sins are all that you need on your way to heaven."*

I could see a large arc of a stage with many ordinary people acting out their lives. Jesus said: *"My people, I want you to be only who you are and not anyone else. Each of you has unique talents and graces which are to carry out a mission that only you are to accomplish. Do not put on airs of someone important or try to hide from doing your mission. If you refuse to carry out My plan for your life, then you are wasting the talents that I wanted you to use. Fulfilling your mission for Me is your life's most important responsibility."*

I could see a storage room with large tables and chairs ready for setting up a banquet table. Jesus said: *"My people, you know of the Wedding Banquet in heaven that I have prepared for all souls being rewarded in heaven. I also have come to the earth to establish My Kingdom. When I came to the earth, I told you the Kingdom of God is at hand. This Kingdom is a spiritual kingdom centered around My Church. The banquet table on earth is the altar at Mass when you celebrate My Eucharist in My Body and Blood that you consume at Holy Communion. You all become a part of My Mystical Body when you receive Me in Holy Communion."*

I could see a liberty bell and it was ringing to celebrate freedom. Jesus said: *"My people, you think that when you live in a democratic society that you have freedoms. It is the will of the majority that directs the laws of your land. This way of government needs checks and balances in order that one group does not dictate its wishes to everyone. The real freedom that you can* have is in spiritual freedom. When your love for Me and your neighbor becomes more perfect, you will not see My Commandments as limits, but only guidelines for living a proper Christian life. You have free will and when you choose to glorify Me before yourself, then you will be living closer to My Divine Will."

I could look up from a deep water well to the blue sky above. Jesus said: *"My people, sometimes you feel trapped by the things and events of all that is in your life. When you try to solve life's problems on your own, you many times fail miserably. But when you look up and pray to Me, you will see the light at the end of the tunnel. What may seem impossible to you, can be possible in prayer and trust in My help. So take courage, My children, and call on My help in every desperate situation and I will lighten your burdens."*

I could see some prisoners in prison and they had a hopeless look on their faces. Jesus said: *"My people, these are real lives of souls that are found in your criminal prisons. They need to be visited and given hope for a new life in the Spirit. There are some who do prison ministry and find it very rewarding to put a spark of life back into these hopeless souls. Unless they see the need to repent of their actions, it will be very difficult to live in society once again. So pray for your prisoners and visit them to give them hope in this life."*

I could see dishes stored in a kitchen and there was a need for peace among families that are always fighting. Jesus said: *"My people, when I came at Christmas, I was bringing peace to all of mankind. I showed you how much I love all of you by My free will choice to offer up My life for all of your sins. My Divine Sacrifice was the needed price for the salvation of all of your souls from your sins. If I could love you so much, you can show your thanks to Me by loving Me and your neighbor. Love in a marriage is the harmony that I want you to bring to this earthly life. In Matrimony you have the grace to love each other and bring children into this world under the marriage bond. Love requires a giving over of yourself for the benefit of the other spouse. It is this willingness to do things for each other without expecting anything in return that will seal love at the center of* the marriage with Me in the middle. It is important to help families stay together as you help your children in their needs. Divorce results from a lack of love and self-giving. To keep a marriage thriving you need loving communication and a common family prayer time. If God is missing in your family, then you are allowing the devil to divide it. Love one another as I love you."

Friday, January 14, 2005:

At St. Josaphat after Communion I could see a priest sacrificing the Mass in front of a blank wall. Jesus said: *"My people, every time that you come to an Eastern Rite church you are awed by the beautiful icons, crucifixes, and mosaic artwork. They have kept the old traditions even if they are different from the Roman Catholic Mass. These people give Me more reverence than many of My Catholic people. In contrast many new Roman Catholic churches have very few, if any, statues and pictures of the saints, no crucifixes with My corpus, and My tabernacle is usually in a back room. Little by little all that is holy, including My Blessed Sacrament, is being removed from My churches. This is because of the Satanic influence of the masons in My church. I have long been warning My followers not to let the New Age symbols and idols into My churches because they have evil power associated with them. If a church continues to place such objects on the altar of the Mass, then leave these churches, even if you must go into the homes for Mass. I am protecting My people from evil influences, but you must discern in the Spirit when you must leave for My refuges. I will give you advice and warnings when you need to know about the time of the great tribulation."*

Later, at St. Theodore's tabernacle I could see someone using a computer virus to shut down parts of the internet. Jesus said: *"My people, there are many people that use the internet for banking, buying things and sending mail. There are also malicious thieves trying to steal identities to ruin people's bank accounts by stealing their money. These computer writers are sending viruses and other malicious software to ruin companies and steal information just because they want to flaunt their skills on ev-*

eryone. *There also are those computer people who take money to try and destroy the internet by terrorist tactics of takeover. It is the control of buying and selling that the one world people are interested in, and they will go to extremes to accomplish it, even if it means bringing down the whole internet. Many are profiting from selling antivirus programs and programs that clean off electronic trails to where you were on the internet. Unless others send out bad programs, no one would have to buy these repair programs. Beware of all that you do on the internet. You need to be cautious of every unknown program that finds itself on computer."*

Saturday, January 15, 2005:
At St. John the Evangelist after Communion I could see some seats at a large football stadium and it was amazing how many people came to these games. Jesus said: *"My people, you have many sports enthusiasts that will come to watch a football game in all kinds of weather. Yet, you find a lot fewer people that want to pray or adore My Blessed Sacrament. Your earthly desires many times overshadow your heavenly desires. You would much rather please your senses than follow your soul's craving to be with Me. During Lent, you have time to evaluate what is more important. Is a short enjoyable moment on earth more valuable than an eternity in the peace and glory of heaven? It is the devil who tempts you to desire sinful pleasures, just as he enticed Adam and Eve to sin. If you worship things and pleasures of this world more than Me, you will die in your sins and be on the broad road to hell. If you desire to be with Me in love in heaven, then you must follow My Commandments of loving Me and your neighbor as yourself. I told My apostles that I came to heal sinners and die for sinners, and not the self-righteous who do not want My healing of their souls. All of you must recognize that you are sinners and are in need of My grace. I am warning you as the time of tribulation comes, that the Antichrist will be a charismatic man of peace who will draw many weak souls to worship him at these same large stadiums. Do not go to see him and avoid looking at his eyes in person, in pictures, or on TV because*

of his demonic powers of suggestion. Do not take his mark or computer chips in the body that will control your mind. At the coming of the Antichrist let your guardian angels lead you to safety at My refuges. There I will protect you from the evil ones and provide for your needs. As the Antichrist reaches full power over the earth, then I will come and conquer all evil and all the evil ones will be cast into hell. You will then see a renewed earth and My faithful will be rewarded in My Era of Peace."

Sunday, January 16, 2005:

At Holy Name after Communion I could see a small cross drifting away on the water and then there was a large cross on the water remaining in front of me. Jesus said: *"My people, this small cross drifting away on the water is like many people who have drifted away from Me and have let worldly things and concerns replace Me. I am the Creator of the world and even of your very lives, so how can you forget Me and refuse to thank Me for all that I have given you? It is bad enough that your love for Me is waning, but even worse, you are mocking My laws by your wanton sin. You are also destroying the earth and your environment with your pollution and manipulation of the plants and animals by altering their DNA. This large cross that remains before you in the water is how I am using water to bring chastisements against those violating My laws. If you will not pick up your daily cross of following My plan for your life, then I will send you many crosses of destruction to bring you to your knees. You can decide to follow Me or not, but the consequences of sin are death and destruction. Repent of your sins and My blessings will return. Refuse Me and you will taste My wrath for your evil deeds."*

Monday, January 17, 2005:

At Most Precious Blood after Communion I could see someone's feet behind a curtain that could have been either an election booth or a confessional. Jesus said: *"My people, when you think about your spiritual life, you do make an election between Me or the world. It is also a secret ballot between you and Me, but your actions make it evident to everyone what you are choosing. If you voted to love Me and seek the forgiveness of your sins, then you will be drawn behind another curtain at your confession. Those, who choose to follow the worldly gods of pleasure and wealth, reject going behind the curtain of confession because it will mean giving up their earthly desires of sin. You are spirit and body, but the most important is the spiritual life which lives on forever after this life. Choose life with Me, instead of eternal death and suffering with the world. I can offer you love and the glory of heaven. The world only offers you a brief pleasure at the cost of eternal hate and fire in hell."*

Later, at St. Theodore's tabernacle I could see the spinal bones of a large animal. Jesus said: *"My people, I am showing you the bones of a spine because I want My faithful to have a strong backbone in standing up for their faith. There are some who are spineless in being quiet instead of outspoken about your sins of abortion, fornication, and homosexual acts. I love the sinner, but your sinful actions offend Me, especially when you know My laws and how you should be living. If you see these mentioned sins in your family, you cannot be quiet, but you must speak out to warn your family members of their sins. If you see souls on the broad road to hell, it is your responsibility to try and wake them up from their sinful habits. Even if you will be criticized and even rejected, you must speak My words of love and forgiveness. If they refuse to listen you, then pray for them and give them good example. If you make some attempts to save them, then you have done your job and it is their responsibility to take action on your words. When you stand up for your faith in public, then My heavenly Father will stand up for you at your judgment."*

Tuesday, January 18, 2005:

At St. John the Evangelist after Communion I could see a large face of Jesus suffering on a cross but it was spiritual and not physical above the altar of a church. Jesus said: *"My people, this vision of My suffering on the cross on the altar is what goes on at every Mass, whether a church has a large crucifix or not. You are seeing My Body on the cross and not just a plain cross, no cross, or a resurrected body, but My suffering Body. Every Mass is a sacrifice of My Body and Blood, and not just a meal of bread and wine. You are to call each Mass a sacrifice that is offered to My heavenly Father for the remission of your sins. This sacrifice of the Lamb of God is what has brought salvation to all of mankind. This also is why it is important to have a large crucifix on the altar to remind the people of My sacrifice at each Mass. My Real Presence of My Body and Blood is being received at Holy Communion and you need to give Me reverence by receiving Me in the state of grace without any mortal sin on your soul. Do not commit sacrilege by receiving Me in sin."*

Later, at St. Theodore's Adoration I could see a poor town of farmers living off the land in a third world country. Jesus said: *"My people, there are many people in other countries who live in poverty with very little to eat. Here in America you are blessed with jobs, food, and good homes. One thing, that is missing in America, is a need to seek the simple life without wealth and many possessions. You are so busy and concerned with making money to get your possessions that you are under constant stress with little time for prayer. Each day you waste too much time on worldly concerns that will not help you get to heaven. You should focus more on a good prayer life, giving alms, and taking time to help your neighbor. Speak to Me in your own words of how much you love Me. By slowing down your fast paced living by not busying yourself every moment, you can have more time for Me in your life. Then you can focus on seeking My forgiveness of your sins, and receive My grace in the priest's absolution for peace in your soul. Live the simple lives of the saints and you will see the true beauty of this life."*

Wednesday, January 19, 2005:

At Holy Name after Communion I could see railroad cars all over and the bare metal wheels after a flash of an explosion. Jesus said: *"My people, you had a train wreck by an accidental side track turned to go off, which could have been accidental or on purpose. Some died and were injured from released chlorine gas. You do not realize how many dangerous chemicals are traveling* on your train tracks that could cause major problems in a city from accidental or terrorist reasons. This vision of an explosion on a train shows you how such an incident could happen at any time. It is also a sign that better security and safety measures are needed in handling explosive cargo. America has many enemies who would want to destroy your infrastructure with their terrorist activities. Beware of more attempts to cause havoc in several cities at once. If you did not carry on with so many wars against people, you would have less reason for them to hate you. Strive for peace in the world without looking to destroy your neighbors. Refuse to listen to the voices of the one world people who are calling for constant wars."*

Later, at St. Theodore's Adoration I could see a light as a light tower beaming light all around. Jesus said: *"My people, you know when it is foggy or a blizzard of snow that you need a light for a reference where to go. Otherwise, you would be wandering in the darkness without any direction. My spiritual Light is available to everyone that is blinded by their sins. By calling on My grace, I will show you the best way to heaven and you will not lose your focus on Me. My people also need to be beacons of light to spread the faith where sin is rampant. The desires of the body are blinding people's faith and it is getting harder to wake up the people from their sin. You are seeing a storm of evil actions in war, abortions, and the sexual sins. Pray for the people around you that they may follow your good example and learn more of My love through seeing your prayer life. My faithful are always being watched by your peers, so be vigilant in doing only good deeds so you are not seen as hypocrites."*

Thursday, January 20, 2005:

At St. John the Evangelist after Communion I could see up above me in heaven and there was a ring of saints and angels cheering us on to be faithful to God in how we live. Jesus said: *"My people, I am showing you in this vision how all of heaven is cheering and encouraging all of My faithful in your evangelization efforts to save souls. There are many evils and distractions going on in your society. The saints are your models of a simple dedicated life focused on serving Me in helping others. You are constantly facing a battle of good and evil, so you cannot relax and be lazy in your spiritual life. Prayer and frequent Confession is the constant cleansing that you must be about. Just as you keep clearing out the snow from your driveway, so you must keep cleansing the sins from your souls to keep close to Me in a pure soul. It is not easy to instill this love for Me in people who are worshiping the things of the world. Money and possessions are cold and you will not find My love in them. You must have others see your love for Me and how you love everyone. Then they will desire this love of Me over love of the world. Call on My help and that of the saints to help you in saving souls."*

Later, at the prayer group at Holy Name Adoration I could see a battle cruiser sending off Tomahawk missiles to start another war. Jesus said: *"My people, you are just inaugurating your president for a second term, but you are still deep in an ongoing battle with Iraqi insurgents. Many of your people want your troops to come home, and still other rumors speak of more future wars with other difficult countries that are trying to make atomic bombs. Your Congress and your people need to speak out against these trumped up wars that are not necessary. Instead of killing and running up major deficits, now is the time to speak out for peace and the stoppage of constant wars. Pray for peace, My people, or you will suffer more losses and more destruction."*

I could see some school supplies of notebooks and pencils being sent to help the schools damaged by the tsunami. Jesus said: *"My people, many countries have contributed millions for the tidal wave victims for food, water, and materials for shelter. It is going to be difficult to keep enough aid coming over the years that it will take for reconstruction. Another need is for building schools and supplying the materials needed for writing and teaching. This vision is another dimension of the needs of these poor displaced people. Those, who are receiving this aid, are thankful to all the donor nations. Continue with your donations to reputable help agencies to carry on with this needed help."*

I could see a landing of a satellite probe on Titan, one of Saturn's moons. Jesus said: *"My people, your scientists have sent some startling pictures back to earth from the latest probe on Titan, the moon of Saturn that had the most interesting features. Continuing pictures and sampling of rocks on Mars also are claiming previous water present to form certain minerals in the rocks. You also are trying to hit a comet to see what it is made of. Some of your experiments could alter the course of these bodies that could bring them closer to hitting the earth. This curiosity is not worth the risk of an undesired result. Man has manipulated nature in many bad ways and you are going beyond discovery into changing the world and the universe to your own liking. Beware of the consequences of your bad actions and let things be as I created them."*

I could see a cow that was a part of a farmer's herd. Jesus said: *"My people, there are some strong concerns about spreading mad cow disease after a second case in Canada. Much of the meat of the animals that you eat every day is always subject to disease and passing it on to man. More attention is being focused on protecting your food from disease, but there is much manipulation with the feed and hormones added to grow them fatter. You must be prudent and not adulterate your foods, or you could cause more cancer and other health problems. Try to eat healthy foods and less of them so you do not get overweight."*

I could see a row of houses and there were large amounts of ice forming on them from a severe ice storm. Jesus said: *"My people, your normal winter weather is returning with heavy snowfalls around your lakes and ice storms in various places. I told you that you would see more power outages with winter storms that will bring wind and ice storms to challenge your ability to provide heat and food for your families. Now is a good time to have some extra food and alternate fuel for the times when you may not have your electricity. Prepare now before it will be difficult to survive."*

I could see more flooding and natural disasters from weather related storms. Jesus said: *"My people, I am showing you more floods and natural disasters in your future as you refuse to stop your sinful lifestyles. Many of these chastisements are for sin in certain areas. If you do not repent of your sins, these disasters could worsen. Now is the time to repent and turn to Me for help while you still can change things. Pray for sinners to see My Light to change, and take advantage of this coming Lent for improving your spiritual lives."*

I could see some New Age influences being brought gradually into the churches. Jesus said: *"My people, I have warned you before of avoiding any New Age influences in My churches. Now songs about the earth and various gods of the earth are being introduced in some areas making way for more obvious idol worshiping. It is bad enough that you worship money and possessions instead of Me, but do not take on these Eastern mysticisms of transcendental meditation that worship things of the earth as gods. Pray for My help and discernment to avoid idol worship and only worship Me."*

Friday, January 21, 2005:
At St. John the Evangelist after Communion I could see someone shoveling the snow off his roof. Jesus said: *"My people, now that you are back into the cold and snow of winter, people are having to struggle to eat and stay warm. Dealing with life's trials is at times a test of your physical endurance. With faith and trust in My help you will be able to overcome all the obstacles that may be placed in front of you. You will also be tested by the evil one in your spiritual endurance as well. This battle with sin and temptation is life's real hurdles that have meaning for the direction of your eternal life. Even if you should fall on occasion, you can have grace restored to your soul in Confession to the priest. With Confession available, you have no excuse to not have a soul free of mortal sin. Just as you struggle every day for your physical survival, so you should work even harder for your spiritual survival in keeping your soul free of mortal sin. Mortal sin is death to the soul and you should be driven to Confession to keep your soul alive in My grace."*

Later, at Terry's house during the rosary I kept seeing visions of people enduring the cold winter weather. Jesus said: *"My people, you are experiencing some very cold weather and this is a sign for you of all the icy cold hearts who are far away from Me in their sins. I am warm and My Baptism of fire inspires you* with My love and helps you to come closer to Me in this cold world. It is love that is missing in your hearts both for Me and for others. If you are to follow My Commandments, you must have this love in your hearts, minds, and souls. So I am inviting everyone to come to My graces and turn your stony cold hearts into hearts of warm love that you can share with Me and your neighbors. The coldness of sin in your world is represented in your cold weather. So when you gather together in your prayer groups, your hearts will be burning with My love, just as the disciples on the road to Emmaus were when I explained the Scriptures of My coming. Now you are preparing for when I will come again in glory."*

Saturday, January 22, 2005: (Roe vs. Wade Anniversary)
At St. John the Evangelist after Communion I could see an aborted infant under the ground in a proper burial place. Jesus said: *"My people, I have shown you many graphic representations of your grisly killing of unborn children. This vision of a tomb for a proper burial is more than you are acknowledging of the human dignity of each conceived life in the unborn. I showed you stony icy cold hearts before, and this also relates to your cold blooded killings of the unborn. The numbers of your abortions far surpass all of those killed in your wars. How can you deny the humanity of each unborn child? At conception all of these fertilized cells have a soul and an angel bestowed upon them, so that taking this life is against My Fifth Commandment of 'Thou shall not kill.' It is the angels of these killed infants that are witnessing this carnage to Me. You cast these dead unborn infants into garbage containers and do not give these little ones an honorable grave. How callous your people have become in keeping this authority in your laws to allow the killing of My children. Unless you stop your abortions and repent of these mortal sins, your country will be brought to your knees through continuous disasters and the ruination of your civilization. Choose life, or you will choose death and its consequent destruction."*

At St. John the Evangelist Adoration I could see someone using an ornate fan representing polite society. I then saw a banker's old desk for settling accounts. Jesus said: *"My people, there are those in your society that do not want to be confronted with their sins of abortion. So when you show them models of the size of the infants that they aborted, or more graphic bloody pictures of the suction abortions, they are appalled and want to put you in prison. They cannot face the reality that they killed their children, and they become angry at you because they want the right to kill their unborn infants. Every time that you protest abortions, you receive this backlash from women demanding their rights to kill their babies. In My eyes these mothers have no rights to kill, and everyone, who has an abortion, will have a heavy reparation for this premeditated murder. The vision of the banker's desk for settling accounts is a reminder at your judgment of how you will have to settle accounts with Me for the taking of any life. This is the most serious mortal sin that you could commit in taking another's life. You can be forgiven in Confession, but you are denying My plan for this life. At your death or at your Warning experience, you will see what this person, that you killed, would have accomplished in their mission for this life, but you cut off My plan. Pray for the mothers to not have abortions, and it is your Christian duty to speak out publicly against abortion."*

Sunday, January 23, 2005:

At Holy Name after Communion I could see some large drawers with handles stacked four high. Jesus said: *"My people, you have read in today's readings of how I called My first disciples from their fishing boats. I told them that with Me they would be fishers of men. My calling is received differently by various people. This vision of four drawers is likened to how people receive My call and My Word. In the parable of the sower (Matt.13:3-9) some are like seed thrown on the footpath where the birds eat it up, as when people hear My call and they cannot accept My commitment. Others are like the seed thrown on rocks that sprout and wither for lack of roots. These hear My call with rejoicing, but they are not persistent in following Me because of their lack of faith. Still others are like the seed that falls among thorns that become choked by the cares and comforts of the world. Finally, there are those where the seed falls upon good soil that yields a hundredfold, sixty fold, and thirty fold. These are My faithful people who hear My call for their mission and drop everything to come and serve Me without reservation. Within My faithful some are called to be priests and deacons. Some are called to be prophets or evangelists. As some are called to be leaders, the rest are followers of My Church. All of My disciples are baptized and called to save your soul and the souls that you meet in life. Even if you are not a leader in My Church, you can still be a beacon of faith to bring souls to Me. Heaven rejoices for those who willingly accept My call and use their talents to fulfill the mission that I have given them."*

Monday, January 24, 2005: (St. Francis de Sales)
At St. John the Evangelist after Communion I could see a beautiful ornate design on the aisle going up to the altar in a church and there were stained glass windows on the sides. Jesus said: *"My people, your priest talked of St. Francis de Sales' teaching that everyone should be seeking perfection to gain heaven, and not just the religious. Even in My Gospel I have instructed My faithful to be perfect as My heavenly Father is perfect. (Matt.5:48) This striving for perfection in your spiritual life can start with fasting and daily prayer. You are not far from the beginning of Lent when you can focus more clearly on bettering your spiritual life. Going to daily Mass and Holy Communion can give you the added grace to work toward your perfection. I know that you are weak in your sinful nature, so a frequent cleansing of your soul at Confession will also help you to perfect yourself with a pure soul. Love Me and your neighbor as yourself, and you will have a life's work to follow Me in holiness."*

Later, at St. Theodore's tabernacle I could see a bell sounding and hear a siren going off as at a fire station. Jesus said: *"My people, I am doing everything to get people's attention to listen to Me, but many are too wrapped up with their worldly pursuits that they have turned My message of love away from them. I want to remind you of what happened to the rich man who tore down his* old smaller bins to build new and larger ones to hold all of his harvest. Yet, he was a fool because I called him home in death that night. If you store up riches only for yourself, to whom will they go when you pass on? The things of this life come and go in a short time and your life will pass you by until suddenly it is your own moment to die. Since you are only here for a brief time and you do not know how long you will be here, then live the present moment in sharing all that you have with others. When you have true love to help someone, you do not look for something in return. When you give alms freely, even tithing ten per cent of your income, you will gain more in heaven than what your money could buy you in possessions. In like manner you should be willing to share both your time and your faith in helping to save souls for Me. The more souls, that you bring to Me, the more merits that you will gain in heaven for your judgment. I want My faithful to be reverent to My Blessed Sacrament, and be persistent in working to improve your perfection. You should also be persistent in seeking to save wayward souls. Once you understand the beauty and greatness of My love, how could you ever refuse to serve Me? Love is My most important message because I died for all of you out of love for you. Those, who are saved, will receive a joyous reward in heaven that will be beyond your human comprehension."*

Tuesday, January 25, 2005:
At St. John the Evangelist after Communion I could see some footprints tracked in from the snow outside. Jesus said: *"My people, I am showing you these footprints as a reminder that I want you to walk in My footsteps in imitating My life. If you are to be a Christian, then people should be able to see that you are one of My followers by your actions. You have read in the readings about the miraculous conversion of St. Paul to being one of My greatest missionaries of the faith. Very few conversions happen with such a flash of light, but the reaction to following Me in love has been a reward to many people. Many converts to the faith are stronger in their devotion to Me than those who are born into the faith as an infant at Baptism. Even though you*

may be baptized, you still need to make a personal commitment of your life to My service. I talk of many lukewarm in the faith who give Me only lip service without love in their hearts. Many have received My Word, but they have not yet acted on it. Unless you accept Me as Savior and seek the forgiveness of your sins, you are not headed on the narrow road to heaven. I have called everyone to repent of their sins because the first step of conversion is accepting that you are a sinner and are in need of My grace. Baptism and Confession cleanse the soul of sin and this is your way to saving your soul. Baptism and Confirmation also call My followers to be evangelists in spreading My Word of love to save souls. I died for all of mankind to have your sins forgiven, but you must make a forward step to accept My gift of salvation in repenting of your sins. Follow Me in My footsteps throughout your life, and you will be on the right path to heaven."

Later, at St. Theodore's Adoration I could see a large building and a large symbol of a nucleus and three electrons traveling around it to indicate radioactive substances. Jesus said: *"My people, you already have been challenged in Boston with a false plot to set off a dirty bomb by your news reports. You will see more and more potential for terrorists to set off a nuclear device in one or several of your cities. In some populous cities this could kill many millions of people. The reaction from such an attack could cause a nuclear conflagration against Arab countries or other countries that could even endanger man's own survival. This can be mitigated by prayer and repenting of your sins. War and hate will only result in more wars and killing, so America needs to make peace and leave Iraq or worse things will befall it. The militant terrorists keep telling you that the next attack will take many lives, so you should be prepared for even a nuclear attack. Pray for peace that such weapons of mass destruction are not used, or World War III could break out."*

Wednesday, January 26, 2005:
At St. John the Evangelist after Communion I could see several babies in a nursery. Jesus said: *"My people, remember when you went to the hospital to celebrate your newborn daughter, or son,*

or grandchild. There was great excitement and anticipation to see a new life come into the world. The parents and the doctor were all smiles together. Now contrast this with your abortions and how your culture of death tries to hide these gruesome killings by calling them fetuses and only tissue to dehumanize these babies. All abortions kill a human life, and there can only be sorrow and guilt for these mothers who kill their children. The doctor also shares in this guilt by accepting his blood money as just a business. How can Americans endure the millions of babies that you have killed? Even I cannot endure your killing of My little ones only for your own earthly convenience. Do you think that I will forget these killings? I tell you they will witness before you at your judgment. You can be forgiven in Confession, but there will be a heavy reparation for this sin as individuals and as your country. Pray for mothers to stop their abortions, and that America will change its laws that allow these killings. America will pay dearly for all of your abortions, and even worse if you do not stop your abortions."

Later, at St. Theodore's Adoration I could see a switch for turning a machine on and off. Jesus said: *"My people, life can be lived normally according to My laws, or out of the norm according to man's laws and desires. Why is it that many choose to live together in sin without marriage, in divorce, or in homosexual relationships? I made you male and female to live normally in marriage, but man desires freedom to have pleasure, even if it means violating My laws. Living in sinful relationships is a source of constant sin and you need to examine your spiritual relationship with Me. If you desire heaven and want to love Me, you will need to follow My Commandments and live a life of commitment in marriage if that is your calling. You can live a single life, but without fornication or masturbation. Living a normal life without sexual sins is the desired path to heaven. It may be difficult to avoid a sinful lifestyle, but it is purity in your soul that is far more valuable for your spiritual life. You may fall at times, but you can refresh your soul at Confession. So focus your way of life to please Me and not your selfish desires of pleasure. Living a life of consecration to Me and a loving commitment to your spouse will give you a much more satisfying way of life. When your love is focused on Me and others more than yourself, then you can fully share your life without any misgivings or holding anything back. Love means that you want to give of yourself to Me and your spouse without expecting anything in return. The more perfectly that you have love, the easier it is to follow My laws of love. You always have My love, and I am always seeking your love in return."*

Thursday, January 27, 2005:

At St. John the Evangelist after Communion I could see a very narrow entrance into a building. Jesus said: *"My people, this narrow opening represents the difficulty that man has in opening up his heart in the love of forgiveness to those who have wronged him. You have offended Me by your sins many times throughout your lifetime, yet when you sought My forgiveness, I have given it to you out of My infinite mercy. Even when you offend someone or damage their property, you want their forgiveness and are willing to make amends. Anyone can make a mistake, but how big is your heart when someone seeks your forgiveness. Your human sense of justice is very exacting, and you sometimes even seek more reparations in money for someone's offense. Look at how much you sue someone for the least little infraction, and you will see how cruel your justice system is. But once restitution has been made, you still have grudges without forgiveness. You need to let go of all the hurts that people have done to you, even if it is unjustified. I want you to love everyone, even your enemies or those who hurt you. The more you harbor grudges and hate, the less loving you will be. If you die with these grudges of not forgiving people, you will have to make reparation for them in purgatory. In order to come to heaven, you must have pure love in your heart. Forgiving people is very difficult to man, but you must ask My help to have a more forgiving heart. This is just one more thing that must be cleansed on your road to perfection in heaven."*

Later, at the prayer group at Holy Name Adoration I could see a large apartment complex with many units. Jesus said: *"My people,* there are many people who are worried about renting or keeping up their payments on their homes. Life has challenged many households with job layoffs and an economy that has been shaky with deficits and wars. I keep telling people to have trust in Me and I will provide for their needs. I feed the birds and dress the lilies of the field, so I can find miracles to help each of you. The uncertainties for your country are a result of your own actions in abortion and your sexual sins. All of your troubles have come as a result of your own greed and your unnecessary wars. Pray that your people will find shelter and jobs to feed your families."

I could see a family in an older used car. Jesus said: *"My people, I have told you that your standard of living would be decreasing as your manufacturing jobs leave and you are left with lower paying service jobs. You will have to cut back in your family budgets for expensive new cars and be satisfied with less expensive homes. The middle income wage earners will suffer more losses as you will see more of two extremes of rich and poor. Your country is wasting away financially just as your poor morals are dragging you down spiritually as well."*

I could see some purple vestments for Lent and people preparing for Ash Wednesday. Jesus said: *"My people, your Lenten Season is not far away and just as you chose New Year's resolutions, now you can plan some penances to help improve your spiritual life. Fasting, prayer, and almsgiving comes to mind as well as more focus on the cleansing of your sins at Confession. Some may have difficulty with doing a little penance, but it is good to deny some of your sinful pleasures. Take on a little suffering so you can share in what I suffered on the cross."*

I could see people wearing very warm clothes to bear the hard cold winter. Jesus said: *"My people, your winter storms are a real test of your endurance. No matter where you live, you are being tested by many natural disasters. In winter the Northern states suffer from cold and snow. In the fall the South suffers from hurricanes. In the spring the center of your country suffers from tornadoes. In the summer the heat and dryness causes fires out West. Be grateful that you have resources for plentiful food. You are blessed with many riches, but your sin is corrupting your lifestyles. Come to Me more in prayer to balance the scales of My justice."*

I could see some digging for a basement of a new home. Jesus said: "My people, your numbers of new homes have been high because of your artificially low interest rates. As rates increase and inflation picks up, there will be more problems in financing these new homes. Debt levels for governments and individuals are going to be tested with a shortage of funds and the value of your currency will continue to decrease. Many of your financial problems are coming from greed for possessions that you cannot afford."

I could see a time of Adoration of the Blessed Sacrament, but only a few adorers were present. Jesus said: *"My people, it is very difficult in your busy world today to get Perpetual Adoration started and even harder to maintain all of your hours. Those, who are faithful to their hours of Adoration, receive many graces and blessings that they do not realize. When you are before My Blessed Sacrament, you have your very God and Creator right in your midst in the Sacred Host. Even the few that manage to make time for Me are helping to atone for the many sins of the world. Adoring My Blessed Sacrament may seem very simple, but My Host is one of your strengths and weapons to battle the evil of your day."*

I could see a long row of prison cells. Jesus said: *"My people, many of your prisoners of crimes have been in the lower levels of your economy, but your future detention cells will be filled with patriots and religious people. These are the ones that the one world people think will cause them the most trouble in bringing about their new world order. These rich leaders want the masses of poor with little education so they can control them like cattle. If you refuse to be controlled by New Age thinking and the mark of the beast, then they will try to throw you into prison or insane asylums to silence your objections. During this coming tribulation, you will have to flee to My refuges of protection so you will not be controlled by the Antichrist. Be patient for I will come and conquer all evil and renew the earth in My Era of Peace."*

Volume XXXVIII

Friday, January 28, 2005: (St. Thomas Aquinas)
At St. John the Evangelist after Communion I could see a sky scene with beautiful bright colors all along the horizon. In one section I saw the Blessed Mother with saints and angels around her. In another scene I saw Jesus on His throne again with the beauty of angels and saints in heaven. Jesus said: *"My people, every time that you receive Me in Holy Communion worthily, you are joined with all the saints and angels of heaven in My Mystical Body, even though you are on earth. Receiving My consecrated Host is a little taste of heaven at every Mass. This vision of heaven is to*

be shared with everyone so they can realize how beautiful and glorious their eternal life can be with Me. My love and peace will surely give you the eternal rest that you are seeking. This life is a difficult suffering to endure your test of faith among many earthly temptations. The most important things in this life are those means that help you to eternal life in heaven. When you pray, fast, or adore My Blessed Sacrament, you are united with Me in Divine love. I ask all of My faithful to serve Me and consecrate everything that they have over to Me. Do not let attachments to all that is earthly come between us. All earthly things are temporary and are passing away, and that is why you need to be desiring only heavenly things. Those, who choose not to follow Me, are risking the eternal fires of hell. That is why every soul is important to Me and I seek each soul until its dying breath. I also am inspiring My faithful to reach out to evangelize as many souls as they can to bring them to Me and away from the devil's clutches. Be persistent in pursuing every soul as I do because you would not want to lose anyone to hell. Many souls are lazy and spiritually in a daze among the pleasures and attractions of the world. Pray for souls and give them good example in your actions and in your love for Me and others. Your reward for being faithful to Me will be eternity in heaven which demands perfection in holiness."

Later, at Immaculate Conception, Fitzburgh, Mass. after Communion I could see a small stream of water running right through a house that represented the 'Living Water' of God. Jesus said: *"My people, I bring you 'Living Water' that is My grace that runs throughout your whole life. In life water is necessary for your very survival. Without water your crops cannot grow. You are made up of mostly water and you need water every day for your nourishment. Fresh water is very important and My pure rain from the sky constantly replenishes the soil and fills your reservoirs. I remind you of the woman at the well. I told her that she could receive My 'Living Water' and she would not have to draw it every day. I spoke to her of My grace that is just as necessary for her spiritual life as water is needed for her physical life. This vision of My 'Living Water' running through a house represents*

My flowing graces that are always available to you when you ask Me for them. In every sacrament you receive My heavenly graces. In Confession I forgive your sins and I replenish your soul with sanctifying grace. When you receive Me in Holy Communion, you receive My grace to heal your sins and strengthen you against temptations. So when you want to seek heaven, you must follow My Will and My Commandments and I will give you My 'Living Water' of grace so your soul can be alive and vibrant until your death. Keeping your soul pure in grace should be your goal. Those, who have mortal sin on their souls, are in spiritual death and lacking all grace. That is why you need frequent Confession to seek My forgiveness of your sins and renew your 'Living Water' in My graces. I am like a spiritual oasis with abundant graces and 'Living Water' to satisfy the spiritual thirst in your soul. Come to Me always in everything that you need and I will provide for you."

Saturday, January 29, 2005:
At St. Bernard's, Fitzburgh, Mass. after Communion I could see Daniel in front of the hungry lions, but the grace of God protected him and he had no fear. Jesus said: *"My people, in the Gospel My disciples became fearful of the tossing of the sea, even though I was sleeping on the boat. When I calmed the sea and the wind, they wondered what kind of man I was that even the sea and the wind obeyed Me. My disciples still had to recognize My powers as God's Son and even more they still needed to have trust and confidence in Me as I was with them. This fear of things and people of the world is still among you in your humanity, but you should have no fear because I am always watching over you, just as I take care of the birds of the air. This vision of Daniel among the hungry lions takes your faith even one step further in trusting in My help. Do not be timid in speaking out about loving Me and standing up for your faith and My Commandments, even if you may suffer criticism or persecution. As time draws closer to the tribulation, you will even be risking your life in martyrdom to witness to your Lord. Better to be strong and die a martyr's death than deny your faith in Me. You are being tested in little ways*

now, but if you cannot stand up to testing in the green of mild persecution, how will you stand up to testing in the dry of tribulation time. You cannot fight these principalities and powers of evil alone, but you must call on My help in trust that My power is greater. I chastised My disciples for not having trust in My protection, so do not disappoint Me in your own trials. By being faithful to Me even against the powers of evil in the world, you will win your crown of sainthood in heaven."

Later, at Bethel House, Fitzburgh, Mass. after the rosary I could see some jets either doing reconnaissance or taking spy pictures over some new target countries for starting another war. Jesus said: *"My people, the powers behind your government are scouting for their next war. They cannot tolerate peace because they like to stir up constant wars over nothing in order to make money on arms and the taxpayer's debts. Your Congress should stand up and vote no against any future wars, but they are succumbing to lobbyists paying them off or giving them contracts to their states. Do not be surprised when your Congress will again give your military the go ahead under some pretext to attack more countries that need regime changes of leadership. You are in a constant cycle of wars that do not benefit you in any way, yet your leaders are cajoling your people into these wars. Killing and destruction do not solve anything. Then America spends millions more repairing the damage and replacing the government. These constant wars have only one purpose, and that is to neutralize your armed forces and bankrupt your country so the one world people can take over. The American people need to protest against your war makers and strive for peace with no killing. If you sit back and let these wars continue, these evil ones will destroy your country. The devil is behind stirring up wars and continuing abortion, so you need a major prayer and fasting effort to stop this killing. If you do not listen to My words, you will be doomed to repeat the history of nations who have self-destructed."*

Sunday, January 30, 2005:
At St. Bernard's, Fitzburgh, Mass. after Communion I could see an empty chair in a prayer cell. Jesus said: *"My people, I have*

talked to you many times of praying in your room or in front of your home altar. *Your prayer life is a way of communicating your love to Me both in formal prayer and informal prayer from the heart. You pray for your petitions and to give thanks to Me for all the gifts that I have shared with you. Prayer and fasting are a way of purifying your soul as well as refreshing your soul with My grace. When difficulties come into your life, you can ask Me in prayer to sustain you and lighten your burden. This is why daily prayer time is a necessity for you on your road to heaven. Just as I ask My followers to tithe ten percent of their income to charity and support of My Church, so you can also tithe ten percent of your time to Me in prayer and good works. You have been given enough money and time so that you have a Christian obligation to share both with Me and your neighbors out of love. The more that you give in your contributions of money and time, the more treasure that you will store up in heaven. You will be beginning your Lenten Season soon, so now is a good time to put these goals into your life of sharing ten percent of your income and ten percent of your time."*

Later, at St. Camillus' Perpetual Adoration I could see a white monastery sitting on a cliff of white rocks and in the valley below there was a dark fog. Jesus said: *My people, this top of a hill and the valley below are a sign of the ups and downs of life. The monastery is also a source of traditional worship of God, while the valley in its darkness of fog represents the evils and trials that you must suffer through in life. While you are with Me at Adoration or receiving Me worthily in Holy Communion, you feel My comfort and you are protected. While you are on the top of the mountain as My disciples were at My Transfiguration, they did not want to leave, as you desire My peace to go on forever. But this life has trials of testing your faith and you must endure them. You do not have to endure them alone because you can call on My help and strength to get you through. At times your faith is weak and you think that your trials are impossible to bear. But remember with God, all things are possible. All of the spiritual graces, that you gain while you are on a spiritual high, are sufficient in faith to carry you through any valley that you will face in* this life. *The devil will test you with fear and he will try to break your confidence and trust in Me. So do not let the trials and disappointments in this life get you down that you fall into despair. With Me at your side, you have all that you need in this life. When you feel down, call on Me to uplift your spirits and your joy will know no end, even in this life as well as the next."*

Monday, January 31, 2005:

At St. Bernard's, Fitzburgh, Mass. after Communion I could see a crypt in the church and it became a place of hiding in caves from the evil ones. Jesus said: *"My people, in the first reading you read of how the early prophets were abused and killed. Many of them were forced to flee and hide in caves and out of the way places for protection. For now you see Masses said in the crypt or basements of your churches. In the future you will have to go to your homes for an underground church and Mass. Persecution for your faith will again prevail in your world that grows more evil every day. Once the evil ones seek you out to kill you, you also will have to flee like the early prophets for a place of safety. Some in hilly areas will be led by their guardian angels even to caves as refuges. I will protect My people at My refuges where they will not find you. Take warm clothes with you and I will provide for your needs. Some of My faithful will be martyred for My Name's sake, but those remaining will find My protection. Rejoice when you see the Antichrist take control, because you know that I will come soon to vanquish all evil and renew the earth with My Era of Peace. Have trust and hope in Me always as My victory and power are greater than the evil ones who will be cast into hell."*

Later, at Bethel House, Fitzburgh, Mass. after the rosary I could see Jesus suffering on the cross because of our sins. Jesus said: *"My people, I suffered so much on this earth because I had a world of people to save. I suffered here for your sins, so in imitating My life you must suffer also in carrying your own cross. Many seek riches and pleasures to be comfortable in the body, but do not be misled by affluence and power, and do not worship anything before Me. Some make possessions and pleasures their* gods, but it cannot be that way with My disciples. It is harder for the rich to be saved, and that is why I want you to live simple lives. If you are not suffering or doing penance, then you could be enticed to follow the body's desires. You must detach yourself from earthly desires if you are to gain heaven. So the more prayer, fasting, almsgiving, and good deeds you perform, the less time the devil can tempt you if you are spending your time idly. Keep focused on Me in all you do and pray for My help in all of your projects, then life will be less burdensome in My service. Every morning that you wake up, greet Me and be joyous that you have another opportunity to carry your daily cross closer to your goal in heaven."

Tuesday, February 1, 2005:

At St. John the Evangelist after Communion I could see a ladder going up out of a house into the bright sunlight. Jesus said: *"My people, this ladder going up into the sunlight represents your daily struggle on your way to following Me to heaven. Each day brings you one step closer to your death and judgment day. Climbing a ladder is how you have to endure your daily trials, but with faith and trust in Me you can work toward one day entering heaven. This light draws you to Me as I show the way to heaven through love of Me and your neighbor as yourself. You have two choices: one to climb the ladder to heaven by your good actions, or stay at your current level in the world and risk eternity in hell. If you desire heaven, you must also be working on this ladder to improve your spiritual perfection. Following My Will and My Commandments in serving Me is against your earthly nature which seeks to please the flesh. Focusing on Me, as the soul does, will always be a battle with the body. I give you sufficient graces in My sacraments to have the spiritual strength to overcome earthly temptations. Even if you fall in sin, you can be refreshed and forgiven in Confession. All souls are called to My Light, so live in faith and trust in Me and you shall have your heavenly reward."*

Later, at St. Theodore's Adoration I could see a group of people praying the rosary at a prayer group. Jesus said: *"My people, re-*

member that I told you where two or more are joined in prayer, there I am in your midst. Weekly prayer groups give My faithful a chance to share their faith with each other and balance the need for prayer against man's sins. Many times you are praying for lost souls to return to Me just as when I seek the one lost sheep among the rest. I asked My disciples to pray one hour with Me in the Agony in the Garden. Prayer is necessary to show your love for Me. Your daily prayers for My intentions are helping to bring about many conversions. There is much darkness of evil in your world, but there is a bright Light also in the souls who are becoming holier. Your prayers are powerful in your prayer groups, so do not lose hope even when your numbers are fewer."*

Wednesday, February 2, 2005: (Presentation of the Lord)
At St. John the Evangelist after Communion I could see someone wearing a ring with a large jewel on it. Jesus said: *"My people, you see many wearing rings to mark special days in their lives as wedding rings, and rings for high school and college graduations. It was a special day in My life when I was presented as a first born male to the Lord. The offering of turtle doves is a prefiguration of when I would be offered up on the cross for all of mankind's sins. I came into the world as a Redeemer to bring salvation to everyone. I am the new Adam without sin just as an unblemished Lamb ready for the slaughter. Simeon foretold to My Blessed Mother how a sword of sorrow would pierce her heart at My death. Much of this image of sacrifice for the first born son was a foreshadowing of My worthy sacrifice for all the sins of everyone. Consecrating infants to the Lord is what you are doing at Baptism when your original sin is forgiven by My sacrifice. Rejoice that you are now free of your sins every time that you are given absolution from the priest in Confession. I have paid the price for your sins and you should thank Me for your physical life and your spiritual rebirth in My forgiveness."*

Later, at St. Theodore's Adoration I could see an image of President Bush giving his State of the Union address. Jesus said: *"My people, many have heard and seen your president's State of the Union address and there are mixed opinions on many of the is-*

sues raised. It is one thing to speak about your intentions, but it is another in carrying it out with your Congress. In the end it is the life issues around abortion and your unnecessary wars that will determine your country's fate. Many issues around both your tax collection and your expenditures will determine the extent of your deficits. The more deficits you have, the harder it will be to keep your currency from dropping in value. Some hard decisions will have to be made to keep your payments viable to retired people as well as their medical expenses. Your time is running out to stop your immoral society from getting worse in its worship of everything but Me. Americans need to express their desires to solve their problems to their leaders and their representatives or they will dictate their decisions upon you. The next few years will determine the direction that your country will go. The further you move away from My laws, the more chastisements you are calling upon yourselves. Keep Me close to you, My people, for I have the words of everlasting life."

Thursday, February 3, 2005: (St. Blaise)
At St. John the Evangelist after Communion I could see the back end of a garbage truck packing away the weekly rubbish. Jesus said: *"My people, every week you go through your house to rid any refuse and garbage to be picked up. Just as you concern yourself with the tidiness of your homes, so you should also think of keeping your soul cleaned up from your sins as well. Each night you could take a few moments to think over any sins that you committed that day and write them down for when you go to Confession. If you have any mortal sins, you should plan to get to Confession as soon as possible so you can receive Holy Communion worthily at Sunday Mass. Seeking My forgiveness of your sins in Confession is similar to removing your trash. Only in Confession you are cleansing your sins to have a pure soul renewed with My grace. People may forget how dirty with sin your soul becomes because you cannot see it as easily as the physical trash in your house. That is why frequent Confession is good to remove your venial sins while you still remember them. All sin offends Me and that is why your coming Lent is a good time to*

root out your most frequent sinful habits. *If you do not have shame in your sins, then some will think they are not committing any sin. Your human nature is weak to sin and only through My sacramental grace can you resist the devil's temptations."*

Later, at the prayer group at Holy Name Adoration I could see a small stone dwelling and then it replicated into many dwellings as far as I could see. Jesus said: *"My people, I have given you the signs of when to go to My refuges which are: a world famine where people will be killing each other for food, a formal schism in My Church, and when people will try to force chips in the body. Some have been concerned about where the refuges will be found, but My angels will lead you. Some are concerned that there will not be enough shelter for you. I assure you that I will multiply the existing houses so that everyone will have a place to stay and call their own. With Me all things are possible, especially in the testing of the tribulation."*

I could see some men getting some rifles for another battle in Iraq. Jesus said: *"My people, the fighting in Iraq has carried on for two years and still your military says it needs to stay longer. Much of America's reserves are being used for several tours of duty because your troops are being stretched too thin in too many conflicts. There are some trying to fan the fires for more wars, but you have neither the troops needed nor the funds available. The American people need to see that constant wars are not solving any problems, but they are killing your troops and causing larger deficits. Stop the wars now before they will destroy you. You need to be peacemakers and share love instead of being war makers that create hate."*

I could see a large metal crucifix on a church altar. Jesus said: *"My people, many of your new churches and renovations are excuses to remove the traditional statues and crucifixes that were on the altars. My tabernacles also are disappearing into back rooms as well. Do not despair when some in authority are changing My worship to do their own wishes. Many directives have been given from the Vatican that are not being followed. These are more signs of the coming schism in My Church. Fear not because I will return things to their former beauty. Trust in Me and pray for My help to protect you."*

I could see order and beauty coming back to Dubrovnik where a church of St. Blaise was rising to beauty once again. Jesus said: *"My people, this church of St. Blaise in Dubrovnik is another example of how war has scarred beautiful churches. Ethnic cleansing by various dictators created much turmoil and killing in this area. Many times My saints had to suffer martyrdom because they would not bend to the current ruler's demands. This will be coming again to test your faith, so do not bend for comforts or money, but stand up to your persecutors."*

I could see some bicycles in a race. Jesus said: *"My people, some will need to use their bicycles to reach My refuges after their cars run out of fuel. You may be in a race to escape the evil ones, but once you arrive at your refuge, your persecutors will not be able to see you. St. Paul speaks of fighting the good fight and finishing the course, and this will apply to your flight to My refuges. Do not fear the evil ones because I will give you the grace to endure your persecution."*

I could see some large pagodas that also were multiplying at a refuge for plenty of shelter. Jesus said: *"My people, you will see many miracles at My refuges. Not only will your dwellings multiply, they will also expand upwards with more floors as in pagodas. These miracles will be beyond the normal earthly possibility, so believe that My miracles will provide for all of your needs just as I did in the Exodus. Pray much that you will have strong faith when evil will test it."*

I could see a large merry-go-round and it was speeding up to show how the signs were close for the Warning to come. Jesus said: *"My people, many keep asking when the Warning will occur, but I continue to not give you dates, but call you to look for My signs to indicate when this will happen. The many trials for obtaining food because of disasters are bringing a potential world famine closer to reality. My pope son's health has many concerned about how long he will live before a division occurs. Many smart cards are being forced on people and some are already taking chips in the body. Since the Warning comes before the Antichrist, so these signs suggest it is soon even by your stan-*

dards. *Prepare for this time by good Lenten devotions that will keep you pure of heart and soul."*

Friday, February 4, 2005:
At St. John the Evangelist after Communion I could see the glass on a picture making a reflection, and then I saw a picture of Jesus. Jesus said: *"My people, this reflection from the glass combined with My image is a sign to you that you must let people see Me reflected in your actions. If you are to be a real Christian, it means that you must imitate Me in your daily lives. You already are made to My image and likeness when you were created in having a free will and the indwelling of the Holy Spirit. You know that I was without sin, so you need to work toward your own perfection in limiting any sinful actions. If you follow My Commandments, you will witness love for Me and your neighbor. If you witness to true love, it will mean speaking only good things about others, and striving for peace in your world by prayer and good actions. Start your own peace movement without any anger or hate among your own family members. Better to add your love to the world than adding to the world's hate and discord. Pray for peace and love among all nations and the stoppage of all wars."*

Later, at St. Mel's Chapel, Sacramento, California I could see a small picture of Our Lord with a crown of thorns on the floor and then I saw a large piece of shattered glass when someone hit it with their fist to enter. Jesus said: *"My people, the image of Me suffering with the crown of thorns is how I suffer for all the sins being committed by those in the world right now. The image of the shattered glass is how those evil ones in the world are striking out at Me to remove My Name from all things that are holy. You are even seeing attacks on My Blessed Sacrament where the evil one is trying to destroy places of Adoration and hide My tabernacles. My faithful need to take a stand in public to witness to My laws as true and do everything to remove man's laws that are allowing abortion and homosexual marriages. Do not condone these evils of your society by your silence. Abortions are taking thousands of lives of infant babies daily and should not be toler-*

ated. Homosexual marriages are a distortion of true marriage between a man and a woman, and such homosexual acts should be labeled as sinful just as fornication is sinful between unmarried men and women. Christians need to speak out on these issues of your day to show love for everyone according to the Word of God."

Saturday, February 5, 2005:
At St. Joseph's Church, Lincoln, California after Communion I could see a procession and people were standing around a casket of someone who had just died. Jesus said: *"My people, do not wait until your death to review what actions you did to witness your faith to others. My Gospel speaks of you as being the Light and the salt of the earth in witnessing My love to those that you meet in love. You can witness My love and peace first in your own families so you can be peacemakers in keeping a loving family. You can show your kindness to other drivers on the road, or to those that you meet in the grocery store or on the street. Your actions do speak louder than your words and your love for Me and your neighbor should overflow in all that you do. If people know that you pray and are Christians, you should not be hypocrites in your actions as people witness how you act. You are constantly being watched by others and you need to give good example in spreading My love. In essence it is not enough to talk about how a Christian should act, but it is how you live your life as a Christian. Do not put on airs of someone that you are not, but be yourself in good deeds and actions, as you are sincere in your heart with My real love behind you. Love one another and My Light will shine through you. If you are following My Will, then truly you will be the salt of the earth."*

At the Holy Family prayer group, Lincoln, California during the rosary I could see a golden door opening. Jesus said: *"My people, this door represents the golden opportunity to use your life to fulfill the mission that I have given each of you. This open door also represents how I want you to keep an open mind and heart to follow the changes in your life to follow Me more closely. When you have a closed mind and a hardened heart to only do your will, then I have a difficult time to bring My graces into your soul. By being open, you can listen to My words of love and make them a part of your life. Love should shine through all of your actions, and it is difficult to improve your spiritual life unless you are willing to change your desires from earthly things over to only heavenly desires. Every day you are given another chance to serve Me in your actions by your daily consecration and commitment to following My Will. Live My life of peace and love, and you will be giving good example to those around you."*

Sunday, February 6, 2005:
At St. Joseph's Church, Lincoln, California after Communion I could see a street light shining brightly at night and then a river of water for cleansing. Jesus said: *"My people, this lamp stand is My Light that dispels the darkness of sin, but it also represents the Light of My followers that I shine through you. In order to be a beacon of faith, you must have your spiritual life in order so that people will see that you practice what you believe. Do not hide your gifts under a bushel basket, but share your gifts of faith and love with others. There are many ways that you can perform good deeds for others in helping them with food, clothing, and shelter. Not only can you send donations of money to the victims of the tidal waves, but you can help with your time in Church organizations. The water that you are seeing is an example to you how you can keep your soul cleansed from your sins by seeking My forgiveness in Confession. You can also encourage your children to go to frequent Confession and daily prayer as a good example. Do not be afraid to witness your love for Me in public, even if you may suffer persecution or criticism. You all should be striving to be evangelists in bringing souls to Me. It is the most important duty in your life to bring your soul to Me, and help save as many souls as you can. Be the Light and salt of My love for all of those around you."*

Monday, February 7, 2005:
At St. Joseph's Church, Lincoln, California after Communion I could see a beautiful dawn of creation and three crosses in the distance. Then Jesus on the cross came closer to me. Jesus said: *"My people, in the first reading you could hear of creation beginning with the first four days. The vision of a beautiful sunrise is an example of My creation and how you should be giving Me praise and thanksgiving for all of My gifts in the world to you. The*

vision of My suffering and death on the cross is My personal gift to you of My life. My Blood sacrifice has been offered for the forgiveness of your sins and the salvation of your souls. Every time that you come to Mass and receive Me worthily in Holy Communion, you receive the gift of Myself in My Eucharist. Again give thanks to Me for My Eucharist and you can show Me your love in return by following My Will for your life's mission. I thank all of My faithful for your staying close to Me and your reward awaits you in heaven."

Later, at Mary Ann and Mario's house, Camarillo, California after the rosary I could see a beautiful upstairs room and then I saw myself walking down into a basement that was not as beautiful. Jesus said: *"My people, this vision of seeing a beautiful room represents how you are comfortable now with all of your possessions. When the time of tribulation comes, you will be led by My angels to a place of refuge. The vision of going down into the basement represents how you will be going into a place of hiding, and you will have to leave your possessions behind you. When you come to My refuges, it will not be as comfortable as you are living now. It will even be more of a rustic surrounding in the wilderness. Do not have fear in this time of tribulation because I will not test you beyond your endurance. Do not worry about how you will be fed or what shelter that you will have. I will protect you from all the demons and evil ones, but you must call on My help and I will provide for all of your needs. Those, who are faithful, will see their reward in My Era of Peace and also in heaven."*

Tuesday, February 8, 2005:

At St. Mary Magdalen, Somis, California after Communion I could see Jesus on the cross in the background and a large globe of the earth with a clock in the middle. Jesus said: *"My people, I am showing you this clock over the earth because you should be more conscious of using your time for My Will instead of selfish things for yourself. Even as Lent is approaching tomorrow, you should be looking at your spiritual life in how you could improve in your perfection. Love of Me and your neighbor is what I am preach-*

ing to you always. *If you love Me, you would do everything to serve Me in doing My Will and using your talents for My greater glory. Many times you are so taken up with your own agendas that you forget what true consecration is all about. Consecrating yourself to Me means that you are giving up all things that are worldly and focus on doing only heavenly things. I must be the reason that you are doing everything and by imitating My life, you will have love in all that you do. During Lent you will be more focused on prayer, fasting, and almsgiving, but let these things have a deeper meaning of doing them for Me, and not just going through the motions. You may give certain things up for purifying your soul. One focus should be around not wasting your time. Maybe you should limit your television time to only one-half hour of only news or a religious program. Maybe you should limit any time on the internet to one-half hour for just answering mail. The extra time you have could then be spent on reading the Liturgy of the Hours, Bible study, or reading about the lives of the saints. Spending time improving yourself on constructive spiritual reading can give you an open mind for moving ahead in your spiritual perfection. Use this Lent to help you grow, and you will have the benefits for the rest of your life."*

Later, at the Gospa Prayer house, North Hills, California after Communion I could see a spotlight and a stadium full of people. I could see a deep well for spring water and then a dove of the Holy Spirit rise over this land. Jesus said: *"My people, this is a place of holy ground and it is consecrated to Me and My Blessed Mother for our service. Many are drawn here for prayer now and even more will be drawn here for protection during the tribulation. This will be a safe haven or refuge for My faithful. You will see miracles to provide water, My manna, and food for you to survive this evil time. You will see shelters enough to provide even for the numbers that you are seeing in this stadium of the vision. The vision also shows you a spring of water that will be found on this site. The vision of the dove means that the Holy Spirit is sending His graces and blessings to protect this holy ground from all demons and evil people. Those, who will be seeking you, will not be able to see you. Rejoice, My people, that many refuges of protection are being raised up for My faithful in your call to Me for help against the evil ones. Be patient that as this darkness will have its hour, I will then come in glory to defeat Satan and bring about My Era of Peace."*

Wednesday, February 9, 2005: (Ash Wednesday)
At the Luminous Cross, Thermal, California after Communion I

could see a beautiful waterfalls and then I saw Jesus carrying a crucifix, and He gave it to me to kiss His feet. Then a great peace and calm came over me as I was called closer to His service. Jesus said: *"My people, I am happy that you are coming together here at this miracle of My cross to My sacrifice of the Mass. Give praise and glory to your God for sharing this miracle on the Third Anniversary. This Lent will be a very important time of preparation spiritually because your time before the coming tribulation grows short. This world is in a moral crisis of faith because many are falling away from Me. You must call on Me in prayer and My sacraments to strengthen you in your souls to avoid temptation. I love all of you and I am giving all of you Myself in My death on the cross. I raise My crucifix for all of you to kiss My feet and bind all of your sins to the foot of My cross. This miracle of the Luminous Cross is to emphasize the importance of My cross in remembering how much I love you. I come to you in every Mass to share My Body and Blood with you in My Eucharist. My gift of My crucifix is for you to come to serve Me in spreading the words of My Gospel. As you look upon My Luminous Cross, see My love for you and return your love to Me. By your good deeds, prayers, fasting, and almsgiving, this Lent can be a cleansing of your sins, especially in Confession. Repent of your sins and work at changing your lives so they are closer to imitating My life of love in everything."*

Thursday, February 10, 2005:
At St. Jerome's Church, Los Angeles, California after Communion I could see a crucifix on a hill and then a shadow of Jesus as He walked the Via Dolorosa to Calvary. Jesus said: *"My people, your focus in Lent should be on Me as you carry your cross through life. I want you to walk in My footsteps, even if it means that you will share in My suffering. You know how much I love you because I died for your sins. You should be uplifted that I have brought you salvation, and My graces are available to all who call on Me. During Lent you are focused on My Stations of the Cross as you follow in My shadow. Fasting and prayer should help you to strengthen your spiritual life. Every day you should*

consecrate everything that you have over to Me. Then every action becomes like a prayer to Me, because you are doing everything for My Name's sake. Be open also to help your neighbors in their needs without being asked. When you help others, you are helping Me in them. Lent gives you an opportunity to grow closer in your love for Me and to think less of your comforts, eating, and your possessions. All of your efforts here on earth can store up treasures in heaven to balance off the reparation due for your sins. Better to come to your judgment with your hands full of good deeds. Show your love for Me by thinking of Me throughout your whole day. Then you will always be focused on your path to heaven."

Later, at Holy Name's tabernacle I could see some heavy wire mesh enclosing a detention center, and then a building that housed a Nativity scene was on the other side of the fence. Jesus said: *"My people, this wired detention center is a sign to you that a police state of martial law is not far off. Many religious people and patriots will be captured and imprisoned in detention centers for not going along with the new world order. A time is here when smart cards will become mandatory and your passports will contain smart chips. As these chips will be forced on the people, you will have to make some hard choices how to use these chips. If you refuse to honor them, you could be arrested or lose your money. This will be the first step before mandatory chips in the hand will be demanded by your government authorities. Again, those, who refuse to take these chips in the body, could be martyred or tortured in detention centers. You would not be condemned for taking smart cards, but you would be more vulnerable to accepting chips in your body if you did. As chips are made mandatory, you will be seeing the time to go to My refuges with your angels to avoid being captured. The image of the Nativity scene is a sign that I will come to defeat these evil ones and renew the earth for My Era of Peace. Pray much to trust in Me and be faithful, and you will share in your reward on earth and in heaven."*

Friday, February 11, 2005: (Our Lady of Lourdes)
At St. John the Evangelist after Communion I could see a picture of a large whirlpool of water draining into a large hole. This was followed by a vision of a black hole and a tornado with deep vortices in all the visions. Jesus said: *"My people, this deep sucking sound into a large vortex of water, as in a whirlpool, represents how fast your country is being drained of its money and military*

capability. Millions of dollars are flowing out of your country in trade deficits because you are allowing your manufacturers to export your jobs and your wealth. Your unnecessary wars of killing are draining so many billions of dollars out of your country that your government is afraid to include it in your national budget. Your budget deficits are setting record amounts and draining further capital to pay the interest on your national debt. These fiscal problems, which you have brought upon yourselves, are sinking your dollar and heading your country into bankruptcy. Unless you stop your wars of the one world people, and control your spending, your country also will be sinking like a large boat going under water. Pray much for your leaders to change their course of action, or you will no longer have a viable country. Repent of your sins, or you will suffer the consequences."

Later, at St. Cecilia's tabernacle I could see a trophy case with red violet velvet inside. Jesus said: *"My people, many are attracted to fame and riches for their own sake, as an idol. Some accumulate wealth for its own sake, while others strive for power and prestige. Some even use others to obtain what they want. It is the stealing and cheating to get rich that can destroy others in the process. It is one thing to help someone, but it is worse to blackmail or threaten someone for money. Some steal identities for taking other's bank accounts or securities. Once you can see how futile and passing this world's wealth is, then you can understand how much more valuable heavenly treasure is. Worldly wealth passes away tomorrow, but heavenly treasure lasts forever and can help you to eternity in heaven. Worship only Me as your one true God, and your soul will always be in My peace and love. Do not let the attractions of this world sway you from your focus on Me."*

Saturday, February 12, 2005:
At St. John the Evangelist after Communion I could see the wheels of a small child's tricycle. Jesus said: *"My people, I want you to be child-like in your innocence and blind faith and trust in Me in all that you do. A child depends on its parents for everything, and you need to see that everything that you have came from*

Me, along with all of your talents to do things. In that same vein you should be thanking Me and be grateful to Me for all that you have accomplished for My glory. If you must boast, you should boast about Me and not yourselves. Give all the credit of what you have done to Me so you can diminish your pride. In the same way of My love you should accept the fact that you are a sinner and in need of My forgiveness of your sins in Confession. Do not think that you are better than anyone else because you may have been given more graces; more will be expected of you than others. You can instruct your brothers and sisters only to help save their souls and not to insult them with your self-righteousness. Do not be hypocrites in your actions, and always give good example to those around you. Lent is a good time to improve your prayer life and see the need to confess your sins frequently in Confession. By becoming closer to Me, you can assure yourself a place in heaven with My grace and My help."

Later, at St. Theodore's tabernacle I could see at least twenty nurses rush from their stations to an emergency. Jesus said: *"My people, I am showing you some nurses rushing to some kind of disaster to help the sick and injured. You could face natural disasters, plagues, or terrorism as a result of your many sins. You have just witnessed the worst disaster in many years with the latest earthquake and tidal waves in the Indian Ocean. A new type of HIV is turning quicker to AIDS and is resistant to current medications. Threats of war and terrorists obtaining nuclear weapons are constantly in your newspapers. Even though there are many chances for these disasters to occur, I will be protecting My flocks at My refuges. At My refuges the angels will protect you from being harmed, so have no fear of the evil ones. Many governments are being manipulated by the one world people in their finances and in making wars. Continue to pray for peace and the lessening of disasters by improving your lifestyles."*

Sunday, February 13, 2005:

At Holy Name after Communion I could see people sitting in a nearly dark room and they opened the door and the window shades to let the sunlight come in. Jesus said: *"My people, during Lent many are found spiritually in the dark of their sins. Unless you open the door and windows to your soul, My Light of grace cannot enter and you will be walking in the darkness. You see the beauty of My creation all about you in the physical world. But you are body and spirit, so there is also a spiritual world of My creation as well. It is this spiritual life that needs the most attention during Lent because many souls are sick and dark with sin. I am the Great Healer of souls in conversions, but you need to let Me into your life so you can have a meaningful love relationship with your Lord. You are all My creations and I love you because I made you into My image and likeness with a free will. It is your soul that is immortal and it will live on past the death of the body. Lent should be a time to get closer to Me in your prayer life so you are pointed on the right path to heaven for love of Me. If you truly love Me, then you should show it in your words of love to Me and how you can help your neighbors. Love for Me should not just be limited to one hour on Sunday, but every hour of every day. Confession of your sins to the priest in the sacrament of Reconciliation is the best start to opening your souls to the Light of My grace. Thank Me for all of My gifts and ask for My help every day to lighten the burdens of your daily trials. Take up your cross daily and follow Me, and I will help defend you from Satan's temptations."*

Monday, February 14, 2005:

At Holy Name after Communion I could see a small ornate fence around a race track. Jesus said: *"My people, I am showing you this race track because many of you run your lives as if you were racing through the day to do as much as possible. It is time to slow your lives down so you could do a few things well and have time for your prayer life. Trying to accomplish a long list of tasks each day may make you feel good, but are all these things necessary to get you to heaven? It is better for the peace of your soul to live a simpler life and not a life of constant rushing. If you are fixed on doing so many things, you will be anxious and worried if you do not accomplish everything. Look to those things that will bring you to heaven first as necessary, and then fill in* with earthly things that you have time for. By slowing down the pace of your living, then you will have more time for Me in your lives. Remember that My agenda is more important than your list of things to do. Better to follow My Will and My agenda than being focused only on the things that you want to do. Do not be selfish with your time by showing Me how much you love Me and how much you love your neighbor."*

Later, at Our Lady of Lourdes Adoration I could see a vision of Our Blessed Mother coming before a young girl. The Blessed Mother said: *"My dear children, the reading tonight and this vision are all about my coming to Bernadette. I gave her many messages, but the most shocking to the people was an affirmation of my Immaculate Conception. Jesus so loved me from the beginning of creation that He prepared me to be without sin so when He would be carried in my womb, there would be a pure heart and soul to receive Him. This was just one more step on His path to bringing salvation to all of mankind. One day you will see this proclamation of My co-Redemptrix with my Son, Jesus. You have also witnessed the death of Sr. Lucia to whom I gave many messages as well. Her passing should be a sign to you of how close that the end time events are. Give glory and praise to my Son for all He has done for you. Continue to pray your rosaries for my intentions for all souls to be saved."*

Tuesday, February 15, 2005:
At Holy Name after Communion I could see a secret tube for transporting people underground. Jesus said: *"My people, you have subways for transporting people underground in large cities. There are also secret cities underground in several parts of your country to protect your government people. These underground shuttles are for influential one world people and government officials. There is a secret group of financiers who finance your country's debts and these central bankers are the hidden controllers and directors of your government. They are causing your wars to be started and your huge deficits so they can reap the interest on your national debt. These are the same one world people who want to take over your country when you go bank-*

rupt. *Your whole financial system is corrupt from its foundations with little or no backing of anything with value. Unless foreigners or these bankers keep financing your debts, your government would be bankrupt. They are blackmailing your officials to follow their orders or they will refuse to support your debts. This hidden government is running your country and that is why you have constant wars and constant huge deficits. Pray that your people and your elected officials take back your country, or you will see America destroy itself."*

Later, at St. Theodore's Adoration I could see the snow melting with puddles in the roads. I then saw a cart that was pulled by horses. Jesus said: *"My people, you may think that it is unusual to see a cart pulled by horses, but a time is coming when your fuel may be hard to find. As more industrial nations compete for scarce energy sources and more nations become involved with wars, your oil supplies will become strained. It takes a number of years to convert over to an alternative fuel and those in favor of perpetuating oil will hold out to use gasoline as the main fuel for cars. There will be a major disruption in your oil supplies and you will see a major effect on how your country will have to deal with this sudden shortage. Your standard of living relies heavily on consuming large amounts of fuel supplies, but when these supply lines are broken, you will see a dramatic shift in your lifestyles. Pray for My help when your country will be dearly tested by wars and commodity shortages."*

Wednesday, February 16, 2005: (Ray Leary's Mass)
At Holy Name after Communion I could see a vision of a younger Uncle Ray reaching out to shake hands with my Uncle Bob in the pew. Uncle Ray gave a few words of how he was sorry if he offended anyone by having his body cremated. Jesus said: *"My people, it is difficult when a loved one dies in a distant city and there is no body at the funeral to come and see. My son, Ray, is in need of your prayers, so you can continue to remember him as you pray for your deceased relatives. As the years go by after a loved one passes, they are not in sight all the time to remember them. That is why when you pray at the Consecration or at Holy*

Communion, it is a good time to remember and pray for all of your relatives both living and dead. I have given you many messages to pray for the souls in purgatory and not to forget them. Then they will pray for you both here and if you should find yourself in purgatory after your death. Love your relatives, and even love them by praying for them after they die."

Later, at St. Theodore's Adoration I could see a tall cross standing over the lands of the Middle East. Jesus said: *"My people, there will always be chaos and fighting in the Middle East for land and power. Oil has been one target, but wars and being in control are constant problems for the Arab people to get along with Israel and those who support them. There are several factions in each country that find it hard to live together. Peace is only a short time before the next conflict. Dictators and Islamic leaders have caused many divisions that make peace almost impossible among the many factions of people. True peace will only be when I come again in glory to conquer evil and bring about My Era of Peace. It will be difficult for today's cities to be like Nineveh which repented in sackcloth and ashes and changed their lives when Jonah told them the city would be destroyed. Because of today's stiff-necked people, it will require My intervention to make things normal again. Rejoice at My coming when the Antichrist will be defeated and My reign will once again be established."*

Thursday, February 17, 2005:

At St. John the Evangelist after Communion I could see some new computer chips being torn apart. Jesus said: *"My people, America has tried to rely on its technical advantages in computer chips and software to take up the place of your lost manufacturing jobs. But as soon as something is discovered, your manufacturers ship the technology out to other countries to be made where many nations do not honor your patent protection. Unless your government stops the tax free distribution of your jobs overseas, you will have fewer manufacturing jobs with a gradual decline in your average pay. More of your people are becoming financially strapped with the decline of good paying jobs, and your middle class will be dissipating. The rich are plundering your jobs and your wealth to make themselves richer, but in the end there will be a massive uprising when your taxes cannot afford to support all of your mandated payments to social security, medical support, and welfare programs. The greed of the rich and the sins of your people are bringing your country to self-destruction. If your people do not change your morals and your bad finances, there is little hope for your future."*

Later, at the prayer group at Holy Name Adoration I could see the pope with his hat on and he was offering a Mass. Jesus said: *"My people, I have asked you in the past to pray for the Holy Father as he recovers from his sickness. His strength and endurance have been a source of hope for all the faithful remnant. All of My people need to carry their crosses as persistently as My pope son. This Lent is a time for strengthening your spiritual life. Do not be lazy, but keep up your prayers and fasting for your Lenten penance."*

I could see a holy picture of the Two Hearts on a wall. Jesus said: *"My people, when you are praying your rosary or reading other prayers, it is good to have a holy picture or a statue in the room where you are praying. That is why it is good to have a crucifix, statue or a holy picture in every room. When you are praying each Mystery, you can look on My picture and tell Me how much you love Me. Prayer is an expression of your love for Me, so stay close to Me and you will receive My reward."*

I could see a crucifix on a staff as a procession was moving around to pray the Stations of the Cross. Jesus said: *"My people, I want you in Lent to make an extra effort to pray My Stations of the Cross on the Lenten Fridays. You are preparing for Holy Week and commemorating My death on the cross when you pray My Stations of the Cross. Concentrate on the words of your prayers and try to apply them to your everyday life. If you cannot pray the Stations of the Cross in church, then at least pray them before your altar with a crucifix."*

I could see some pews at church and there were more people present at daily Mass during Lent. Jesus said: *"My people, some make daily Mass an extra offering during Lent, so it is not un-*

usual to see more people in attendance. *As you come to daily Mass, be thankful that you have a priest to offer Mass every day. Again, continue to pray for your parish priest who gives you My Body and Blood in the Mass and My blessing of grace at Confession. Many times you take the priest for granted, but they are being attacked by the demons and they need your prayers to keep their vocation and a good spiritual life of holiness."*

I could see some steps to climb an electric utility pole. Jesus said: *"My people, at times you have electrical power outages from storms and grid problems. It gives you a helpless feeling to be cold and in the dark during winter. It is also difficult in your spiritual life to be away from the warmth of My love and suffer the darkness of your sins. Just as you are joyous to have the linesman restore your power, you are also joyous when you come out of Confession and you are restored in My love and your sins are cleansed with My grace. I can Light up your life anytime that you can come to Confession, or when you receive Me in Holy Communion."*

I could see the priest giving a homily on the Sunday Mass readings. Jesus said: *"My people, it is good that many parishes are meeting in groups to study the Lenten Sunday readings, and as a result, these readings can be more meaningful to your spiritual lives. This interaction with others can reinforce your faith and help you share your faith with others. By focusing on the readings, you can work along and understand the homilies better. Learning about your faith and studying My Word will help you to grow more in your faith."*

I could see a beautiful statue of the Blessed Mother. Jesus said: *"My people, just as you share your relics of the saints with one another, so it is good to share your holy statues in prayer also. Your rosaries at your prayer group are joined together and there is great power in My Blessed Mother's weapons of her rosary and her Scapular. You were given a great gift in this statue of My Blessed Mother, and you are sharing this gift with your prayer group as well. Give thanks and pray for those who give you such gifts."*

Prepare for the Great Tribulation and the Era of Peace

Friday, February 18, 2005:
At St. John the Evangelist after Communion I could see a clock, it was faceless without numbers. Jesus said: *"My people, this message is about not letting clocks dictate your life. I know you need to think of meal times, bedtimes, and special meetings, but do not fill your day up with so many activities that you do not have time for your daily prayers. If your time is so rushed, then you need to*

set a particular time for your prayers and plan other events around it. There are very few things other than work that cannot be put off to a later time. Try to get your prayers in early, instead of leaving them to the last moment at night when you are too tired to pray. I have given you the gift of all of your time in your gift of life, so the least you can do to thank Me is to give Me some quality time back in prayer. If you continue to put Me off each day with little or nor prayer time, how will I recognize you as Mine when you reach your judgment and there is no more time. Now is a good time during Lent to establish a love relationship with your Lord before your time runs out."

Later, at St. Cecilia's tabernacle I could see a large black pit where people fell into despair and addictions. In another vision there was a land of bright Light and beauty where God rewards His faithful. Jesus said: *"My people, during life no one is spared trials and disappointments, but it is how you deal with your struggles that will point you in your life's direction. Many at some time in their lives have had to deal with lost jobs, deaths, and sickness. There are also good times in your life to raise you out of the valleys. But some do not have a strong faith to trust in Me to help them through their dark moments. Some even let despair and addictions take them over because they cannot stand up to reality. You have friends and relatives who may help you financially, but you need My help and your prayers to get you through life's trials. It is better to have confidence in Me than to trust in your own devices. No matter how bad things may get, you can always come to Me with your needs. With patience all of your troubles are eventually resolved. For being faithful to Me, I will see to your reward both here and in heaven. Do not search beyond your capabilities, but be satisfied with all that I do to provide for your living needs. Even during the coming tribulation I will provide for all of your needs. Rejoice that I will never abandon you, and I am with you to the end so you will never abandon Me either."*

Saturday, February 19, 2005:

At Maximillian Kolbe Church, Mississauga, Ontario, Canada after

Communion I could see Pope Paul II raising a Host and he was protected by glass all around him. Jesus said: *"My people, My pope son, John Paul II, holds Me up at the Mass and he has a great love for Me in My Eucharist. That is why he has encouraged Adoration of My Blessed Sacrament in as many churches as possible. The devil knows the power of My Eucharist and he is doing everything to attack the priests and remove My tabernacles from My churches. You have been assured that the gates of hell will not prevail against My Church. No matter how much the evil one will attack My Church, there will always be a faithful remnant that will be true to My Word. This glass shield around My pope son in the vision is how he is being protected in his health, and his life is being preserved to the proper moment of his leaving which he knows. Even during the tribulation, My faithful remnant will also be protected from the evil ones at My refuges. Have courage and trust in My protection and soon I will cleanse the earth of all evil and renew it. I will then establish My Era of Peace and My love will consume all of you."*

Later, at Neville & Louise's house during the rosary I could see a train going in one direction and cars were traveling out of town in the opposite direction. Jesus said: *"My people, during the coming tribulation some people will be captured and transferred to detention centers aboard these trains. The rest of My faithful people will be fleeing out of the cities in their cars. When you see the signs that I will give you of the world famine, division in My Church, and mandated chips in the body, then you will be led to My refuges by your angels. If you refuse to leave everything behind and go to the refuge, then they will come to your houses to try and force chips in the body on you. You will need to be strong in faith to resist urges to try and keep your possessions and comforts. Learn to not let possessions control you so when you have to leave for My refuges, nothing will hold you back. This is an evil age and the Antichrist will be battling for souls, but you must call on My help to resist him. Trust in Me and I will protect you from the evil ones in miraculous ways."*

Sunday, February 20, 2005:

At St. Joseph's Church, Mississauga, Ontario, Canada after Communion I could see a large number in the thousands of people at a Mass in the Vatican. Jesus said: *"My people, I am showing you a huge crowd of people that have come back to celebrate Mass in the Vatican. Many people will be going back to Mass and the sacraments after My Warning experience. People will have seen Me in My glory and their lives will be completely revealed to them. You will desire to confess your sins in Confession to the priest, and then come to share at Mass. As you read of My Transfiguration, this was a preview of My glory to My apostles in My Resurrection. So My Warning experience will be a preview of My coming in glory to conquer all evil. Just as I had to undergo My Passion and death on the cross for all of you, My disciples had to endure suffering and martyrdom for their faith. My people of today will have to suffer the pain and suffering of the tribulation after My Warning. Some will be martyred and the rest will be protected at My refuges. Rejoice because when the evil ones are defeated, you will share in My mountaintop love and glory in My Era of Peace. Be patient, My people, because this evil reign of the Antichrist in the tribulation must precede My glorious victory. Be assured that My victory will come even when it will seem hopeless. Hold fast and trust in My help and protection at My refuges."*

Monday, February 21, 2005:

At Holy Name after Communion I could see piles and piles of black coal which represented the sins of America. Jesus said: *"My people, I have asked you many times to pray to make up atonement for the many sins of America. I have mentioned them before, but you know they are your abortions, fornications, masturbation, birth control, adultery, homosexual acts and homicides. Your leaders and the one world people are behind your wars against your people and the wars against other nations. All of these sins are weighing against America on the scales of My justice. There is not enough people praying to make up for all of your sins on the other side of My scales. Without repenting of your sins or a changed lifestyle, you can only expect My wrath to fall on your country with disasters, and bankruptcy of your financial system. You have seen other countries like Rome pass into oblivion, and America is on the same path to its own destruction."*

Later, at St. Cecilia's tabernacle I could see a fist as the hand of God sweeping down to strike America. Jesus said: *"My people, I have warned you many times to repent and save your souls from your many sins. You have not heeded My messages of warning and have turned your back on Me to worship your possessions instead of Me. You are seeing My hand of wrath coming swiftly upon you and you now will be tested by more severe natural disasters, financial upheaval, wars, and terrorism. Within a short time you will come begging to Me on your knees to take away these trials. You are beyond the point of no return and soon your destruction will be at hand, just as Sodom and Gomorrah were destroyed. My mercy is infinite, but My justice is being overwhelmed by more sin than can be made up by prayers and good deeds. Your country has chosen the path to its destruction and you will be seeing it destroyed before your eyes. Your greed for wealth, possessions, and pleasures have harvested your sins, and the wages of sin are death. Pray for souls to be saved, even as your country will be no more."*

Tuesday, February 22, 2005: (Chair of St. Peter)
At Holy Name after Communion I could see an umbrella with a wooden handle. Jesus said: *"My people, when your weatherman forecasts rain for the day, you think to bring an umbrella to protect yourself from the rain. In today's spiritual world you are beset by another need for protection, only this is from a reign of evil. The devil and his demons are real and active in this world, and that is why you have so much immorality and so many wars. They are tempting everyone and exploiting your greed, anger, and pride. Your spiritual umbrella is My sacraments of grace and My Blessed Mother's mantle of protection in her rosary. When you are being tempted to sin, you can call on heaven's help in Me, My Blessed Mother, the saints, and the angels. I*

always give you enough grace to endure any trial or temptation. Today's feast day is around the authority that I have given to My Church to guard your souls from error and evil. You are to look to My pope son's leadership in faith and morals. It is this teaching authority of My Church that should unite all Catholics and inspire conversions to follow My way of life. There are various divisions among people that do not want to follow My pope son as leader, yet St. Peter and the succeeding popes are given this authority by My own words in today's Gospel. Pray for unity in My Church and for all who follow Me as Christians. Unity in faith in Me will help give each soul the protection that it needs from the devil's temptations."

Wednesday, February 23, 2005:

At St. John the Evangelist after Communion I could see a loud speaker spreading the Word of God. Jesus said: *"My people, this loudspeaker is how I want you to spread My Word of love to everyone from the rooftops. The message that I give to everyone is to share your time, talent, wealth, and faith with everyone. Your consecration to Me means not only that you give everything over to My use, but it also means that everything you have has been given to you through Me. When you accomplish something, you need to give Me the glory and not yourself. Boasting of yourself shows that you are doing things for your own glory. If you must boast, you should boast about Me in helping you to gain what you have. Pride for fame and greed for more wealth are temptations of the evil one. I call you to the opposite virtues of humility and generosity in sharing. Wealth and possessions are cold and temporary, but your sharing with others shows love for others and your good deeds will store everlasting treasure in heaven. Better to be seen as great in heaven by your good deeds than to be praised by men for your financial success. Remember that where your treasure lies is where your heart lies also. If your treasure is on earth, then your heart desires more worldly things. If your treasure is in heaven, then your heart desires heavenly things."*

Thursday, February 24, 2005:
At the Gospa House, North Hills, California after Communion I could see a vision of a young Maria Esperanza and she was smiling on all of us. I then saw Our Lady and she said: *"My dear children, I am very pleased with your prayers at Mass with my Son, and your many rosaries on this fourth anniversary of this Gospa House. Myself with my Son, Jesus, God the Father, and God the Holy Spirit are watching over this refuge of love. My mantle of protection and the angels are watching over this land also. All of my faithful sisters and brothers who have been faithful in building up this ministry are to be thanked for their labor of love. By witnessing to me and my Son, you all will be greatly blessed with many graces. Continue in your good work as you prepare for my Son's coming victory over all the evil ones. Consecrate your hearts and souls to me and my Son, and continue your prayers for all souls to be saved."*

Friday, February 25, 2005:
At the MOM Conference, Woodland Hills, California during Adoration I could see a monstrance and then the children running around in their innocence. Jesus said: *"My people, I want to focus this message on My Real Presence in My Eucharist. When I instituted My Eucharist at the Last Supper, I told My apostles and My disciples that they were eating My Body and Blood when they partake of My consecrated bread and wine. Even though you hear these words at every Mass, some still have a difficulty in believing that I am really present and these species are not just symbols. Some have had an opportunity to see miracles of My Eucharist in hosts that bleed. These miracles were performed for those that doubted in My Real Presence in My consecrated bread and wine. For true believers in My Real Presence you have a deep reverence for My Blessed Sacrament. I want you to pass this belief on to your children and those who do not believe in My Real Presence. Your God and Creator is present in My Hosts in every tabernacle. I have humbled Myself to be present in My tabernacles, and I desire your love for Me to be witnessed in visiting My Blessed Sacrament so I can talk to your heart. You*

are many times discerning your mission from Me and deciding the direction of your life. Pray about every important decision in your lives and walk with Me in imitating My life. Let your children see that you truly believe in My Real Presence by your frequent visits to My tabernacles."

Later, at the MOM Conference, Woodland Hills, California after Communion I could see the eye of God looking down on all of us with love. Jesus said: *"My people, this Gospel is full of great meaning in your very life in how you live. In one word it is by My love that you have life. I am the Resurrection and the Life, and all life comes about by My creative act of your soul. While you are alive in the body, you are experiencing My gift of life. I have died for all of your sins, so you have salvation by claiming your redemption. My death is the greatest act of love that I could give to all of humanity. You know that My love is infinite and I also love every soul that I created. Even though you have offended Me with your many sins, My mercy awaits your request for My forgiveness. Do not refuse to come to Confession because you think that I will not forgive you. I will forgive any repentant sinner of his sins, but there still may be some reparation due for your sins. You are the one who has received every gift that I could give you. I call on everyone to return My love by sharing your love with Me and My image in your love for your neighbor. Love is the most intimate experience that you have in life, and it is this love of Me and your neighbor that you will be judged on. This beautiful heavenly experience when you receive Me worthily in Holy Communion is how I communicate My love to you. I know your needs before you ask Me, and I am always anxious to reward repenting sinners for loving Me. You need to be humble in consecrating everything to Me and you will be repaid many times over in heaven. The more you experience love in this life, the more alive in the Spirit you will be."*

Saturday, February 26, 2005:
At the MOM Conference , Woodland Hills, California at Adoration I could see a large thick cross on the altar. Jesus said: *"My people, this message is all about how I want My faithful to pick up their daily cross and follow Me. This is especially your Lenten journey as you are more focused on prayer, fasting, and almsgiving. The deeper meaning of carrying your cross is that you should be willing to suffer any trial or temptation for love of*

Me. I will give you enough grace to bear up any suffering that you choose to endure. Even some may choose to take on more suffering for your sins and the sins of others. As you offer up these sufferings, give your complete free will over to My Divine Will, so I can mold your perfection in union with Me. As you reach higher in your faith and perfection, I wish that you would not make any complaints of difficulties or testings in your life. Give all things over to Me so you do not take credit for anything, but you should only give praise and glory to Me for what I have accomplished in your life. The more you take self out of your life and detach yourself from the things of this world, the closer you will be to imitating My life as My true follower."

Later, at the MOM Conference, Woodland Hills, California after Communion I was led on a path to the confessional and to confess my sins to the priest as an example to everyone. Jesus said: *"My people, the Gospel of the Prodigal Son is the most loving touch of My compassion in all of My Gospel readings. You know of My mercy, but you are overwhelmed by the father who forgave his son even though he lived a sinful life and wasted his inheritance. Even in your families it is hard to forgive a daughter or son who may be living together in sin. Just as you love your children even when they have gone astray, so I love everyone enough to pursue their souls to be saved. My people, you should understand how much you offend Me in your sins. There are even those who insult Me by not even recognizing how they are sinning. In this material world of rationalizations it is difficult for people to form a proper conscience where they can judge right and wrong. Do not let your peers encourage you to sin because everyone is doing sinful actions. Look at My Commandments and My Gospel readings to decide if something is right or wrong because My law of love is unchanging. No matter how serious your sins are, if you repent and are reconciled, I will forgive you as the father of the Prodigal Son. As the Scribes criticized Me in eating with sinners such as tax collectors, I told them that sick people need a doctor. I have come to forgive sinners and not the self-righteous. When you see the guilt of your sins and how you offended Me, you also will be drawn to this*

path to the confessional in search of My mercy and My forgiveness. When I forgive your sins and give you absolution through the priest, you will be set free of the shackles of your sins. When you repent of your sins, your soul will again be filled with My grace. Recognize that you are a sinner and are in need of My forgiveness. Do not be spiritually lazy by staying away from Confession. Frequent Confession, at least monthly, is needed to keep your soul pure and available to worthily receive Me in Holy Communion. By having your soul pure, you will always be ready for your judgment when I call you home. Reach out to bring souls to Confession, especially those in your family. Your goal is to save as many souls as possible and keep them from hell. Reconciliation is the sacrament for making peace with your Lord."

Sunday, February 27, 2005:
At the MOM Conference, Woodland Hills, California at Adoration I could see some ornate gold objects placed on the wall as if they were being idolized. Jesus said: *"My people, it is difficult in your society today to help people to conversion because there is such a problem with idol worship that has been put in place of worshiping their one true God. The other problem for people to come to Me is that they do not have true love in their lives. Some people are worshiping their jobs, their status, their homes, or other possessions. Others are involved with New Age idols or even occult practices. Some even worship themselves and everything revolves around self rather than Me. In order for Me to come into your lives, there must be an openness to Divine Love. Without this openness, then souls need others who are praying for their conversion in order for My seed of grace to be planted in them. There are many distractions in your TVs, movies, and media that are broadcasting the worldly message and it can drown out My calling to their souls. My faithful need to be My prayer warriors for their family members and those that they meet in the world that are crying out for a spiritual healing. By your good example, prayer, and fasting, you can lead many souls to worship Me in place of their cold idol worship. Idol worship leaves an emptiness in the soul because the soul cannot find peace anywhere else than in My love. That is why it is so important that the spiritual soul should be in control of the body. Fasting can improve your spiritual life by not allowing the desires of the body to control your life. It is this strong attraction to My love that will be the salvation of sinners. It is My infinite mercy and My compassion to forgive sinners that will lead to conversion. That is why your evangelist mission should be focused on My love and trust in My help to win sinners over to Me. When I open your eyes to the true worship of the Divine, then you will be able to open your eyes of faith to see the mission in life that I have for each soul.*

Put your trust in Me and worship Me only, and you will receive My grace of complete peace and love that is your reward for being faithful to Me. Then you will be able to share My love with others and their souls will be drawn to My love that will save their souls."

Later, at the MOM Conference, Woodland Hills, California after Communion I could see a bucket of water being drawn up from a miracle spring at a refuge. Jesus said: *"My people, I assure you that the coming evil of the tribulation is not just another evil age, but it will be more evil than you have yet to see. It is not a time to be fearful, but a time in which I will give you all the grace that you will need to endure the Antichrist. You will not be able to last through the tribulation on your own, but you must call on My help and My grace to save your souls. I will be protecting My faithful remnant at My refuges of My Blessed Mother's apparition sites, places of holy ground, and even caves in mountainous areas. You will be seeing this time as a modern day Exodus when you will have to leave everything behind so you can be protected at My refuges from the evil ones. At all of My refuges you will see luminous crosses of protection, healing waters at miraculous springs, My heavenly manna from My angels and even meat to eat. Do not complain of how I will provide for you because I will be protecting and saving your souls from the evil ones who will not be able to find you. Some will be martyred, but the rest of My faithful will be protected at My refuges. I have given you this mission for the people to be prepared for the tribulation time. The signs of this time are all about you for those who have the eyes of faith and for those who read My Scriptures that describe these end days. I love everyone and I want all souls to be saved, but I know there will be many who will reject Me and they will choose to follow the evil one. Come follow Me in My Word and be prepared in your soul for this test of your faith."*

Monday, February 28, 2005:
At the Luminous Cross, Thermal, California after Communion I could see a beautiful picture of a white dove and a great Light spread out all around the dove. The Holy Spirit said: *"I am God*

the Holy Spirit and I am sending My gifts of the Spirit out upon all who are here today. You come to this Luminous Cross to find the meaning of this sign, but you are witnessing a presence of the Holy Trinity in God the Father, God the Son, and God the Holy

Spirit. *This is holy ground and all who come here are receiving heavenly graces. Many come out curiosity, but there are also healing graces available here. I place My hand over those who come here and the flame of faith is over each of you. When you bring your petitions for healing to Me, I will heal those who have faith in Me. Many will be healed in their hearts and souls as well as physically. You have witnessed the healing of the leper by the prophet and you will see healers and prophets healing you through My power also. Give praise and glory to your God and Master for all the gifts that I am bestowing upon you. I am placing grace in your souls, but I am also placing My love in your hearts so you will find rest in Me. This heavenly love pervades your whole being and many become slain in the Spirit when they are prayed over. I love all of you and I want you to follow God's laws and Commandments as you worship Me. Give glory to God as you love Me and all of your neighbors."*

Wednesday, March 2, 2005:
At Holy Name after Communion I could see some clouds around a mountain and the clouds drew darker. Jesus said: *"My people, this image of a mountain represents the strength of your faith in My Commandments. The darkening clouds are the coming trials that will test your faith. Wars, natural disasters, and financial trials will be harrying you in the coming years. As the tribulation begins, these trials and that of the evil ones will become an ever increasing burden. You will need all of the spiritual strength that you can obtain through My grace to fend off the evil ones and save your souls. The signs of the end times are all around you and now is a good time to firm up your prayer groups for spiritual support. It will be your friends in faith that will help you the most at your refuges. I will perform miracles of protection at My refuges, but you must have faith and hope in My word of encouragement. Your faith will be tested to the breaking point, but do not fear because I will be in your midst. I will never leave you."*

Later, at St. Theodore's Adoration I could see someone carrying a good sized portable flashlight that had a manual crank to generate light. Jesus said: *"My people, this portable flashlight with the light on is a sign to you of more power outages coming. You have had power outages in the past from ice storms and a grid failure. Most of your power outages have been of short duration, but this time it could be for a good number of days. The need for a crank to keep generating light means that your batteries would run out of power from long usage. It would be well to have such a crank powered flashlight for when fuel and batteries will be scarce to find. Your two previous ice storms have occurred in March and April. Have some preparations ready for some possibly cold weather when you are without power. I am the Light that dispels the darkness and I am giving you this warning so you can have some light without power. Trust in Me for My warnings when you need to prepare."*

Thursday, March 3, 2005:
At St. John the Evangelist after Communion I could see some large beams of wood being put together in constructing a house. Jesus said: *"My people, I am showing you these heavy beams of wood that are used to make a sturdy house. This message is all about how strong your faith will be by how deeply you are rooted in Me. If your faith is shallow, it will be like the man who built his house on sand. When the winds and rains of temptation buffeted his house, it fell in destruction. If your faith is strong and rooted in My Church, then it will be like the man who built his house on rock as a firm foundation. When the winds and rains of temptation come, that person will be saved because his faith was firm as the rock. Do not be weak in your faith and do not give Me just lip service on Sunday. You need a deep fervor of faith to endure the evil ones' taunts throughout the whole week. Build up your strength with daily prayer and always be focused on following Me in your everyday actions. For those who are faithful and persevere amidst this world's trials, you will be greatly rewarded in My kingdom of heaven."*

Later, at the prayer group at Holy Name Adoration I could see a small house being used for a store. Jesus said: *"My people, even though it was a nice change to have your prayer group at the* home, you now can have Me again sacramentally in your midst. This small house is a symbol of living a simple life as I did with the Holy Family many years ago. Even with all of your scientific advances you are still human with a body and a soul. Your worldly distractions may have changed, but you have the same mission of loving Me and your neighbors. You may have more conveniences than I did, but you also have more affluence and possessions to distract you from loving Me. Do not let the worldly things control you so you can give your praise and glory to only Me."

I could see a beautiful bedroom with flowers and many decorations. Jesus said: *"My people, no matter how many ways that you try to make excuses for aborting your babies, they are still being killed by the thousands every day. Your society is focused on pleasure on demand, so it is not surprising that accidental pregnancies are disposed of by your abortion on demand. Science has proven to you that the unborn are human from the day of conception. Still your society wants to dispose of life when it is convenient. Many do not want to face the consequences of their sins of fornication and adultery. All life deserves to be protected, and you are fortunate that your mother did not abort your life. Continue to protest abortions and counsel the expectant mothers to see the value of life."*

I could see some young girls playing with their dolls. Jesus said: *"My people, the young children are precious to Me and I do not want them to be abused in any way. Remember how I said that anyone who harms one of My little ones should have a millstone tied around his neck and be placed in the sea. These lives should be protected because I have a plan for each of their lives. Give good example to them and bring them up in the faith so they can experience My love for them."*

I could see some people inside a small boat with a cover over it. Jesus said: *"My people, not everyone can afford to buy an expensive speedboat or a sailboat. Those in the boat can experience My creation more as they explore the seas. Some people treat boats and second homes as status symbols of their wealth. I am concerned only with how you love Me and help others, and not how much wealth that you have accumulated. Focus more on those means of getting your soul to heaven instead of any worldly concerns."

I could see a splitting of roads at the end of a path. Jesus said: *"My people, I keep encouraging My faithful to follow the narrow road to heaven that is less traveled. Avoid the broad road which appears to be popular for being the easy road that leads to hell. Do not be led astray by anyone trying to take you away from Me. Many are called, but few are chosen because they do not want to give everything up to Me. Unless you come to Me as a repentant sinner, you will be traveling down the wrong road. At the end of this age I will separate the goats into hell, but My lambs will be called into My barn of heaven."*

I could see a nice new room that had been refurnished. Jesus said: *"My people, at times your old things do need to be replaced by newer things. It is one thing to fix something that is old and obsolete, but changing things just to have the latest fashion is more of a worldly desire than a necessity. Keep your focus on living a simple life than spending all of your time and money to have the best looking possessions. If you have excess wealth, then you should focus more on sharing it with others than being selfish in buying things that you do not need."*

I could see some Lenten decorations in the church to focus on devotions to improve our spiritual lives. Jesus said: *"My people, I keep reminding you of the Lenten Season that you are in so you can make the most benefit for improving your spiritual life. Your extra fasting and Lenten penances should be kept up throughout all of Lent. Keep reviewing your initial fervor to improve your prayer life so you can continue your Lenten intentions without falling back into your old sinful habits. Lent is an excellent time to take spiritual stock of how you could be living a more Christian life. If you do not suffer to change your life, then you will not see much improvement. It is difficult to train the body to follow heavenly ways because you have many human weaknesses to sin. If you are not willing to improve during Lent, then it will be much harder to change during the rest of the year. Focus your life more on Me and do not let the body's cravings mislead you."*

Friday, March 4, 2005:

At St. John the Evangelist after Communion I could see some keys being played on a flute. Jesus said: *"My people, just as you have harmony in music when you play the right notes, so you can have harmony in life by loving Me and your neighbor as yourself. If all of your world lived in a harmony of love as I created you, you would not have the wars and injustices that you have today. Many of the problems people have are a result of their greed for money and possessions, and their struggle for fame and power. If you were satisfied with your lot instead of desiring more than you could afford, then you would be more at peace. If you did not waste your time on TV and too many unnecessary activities, you would have more time to love Me. Love takes some effort to establish, but if you are too wrapped up in self and selfish activities, then you will not have time for love. It is how you manage your time and your priorities that will allow you to love Me and your neighbor. Work more in Lent on freeing up your wasted time so you can have more time for loving activities of prayer and helping others."*

Later, at St. Theodore's tabernacle I could see a very fast train traveling through a tunnel underground. Jesus said: *"My people, this fast train through an underground tunnel would be some new technology for fast trains with less wind resistance. It will also be an underground link for various underground cities that are being built away from water and earthquake centers. These cities would be protection from impacts of comets and asteroids, possible nuclear war, or a major volcanic disaster. These undertakings would be expensive, but they could be a possible way to protect humanity from massive disasters. I have mentioned caves before as a means of protection for refuges. A properly vented cave with water and food storage could protect My faithful from the evil ones who will be controlling things on the surface of the earth. Caves also would not allow the evil ones to see you as well. Trust in My leadership to protect My faithful from the evil ones in the tribulation."*

Saturday, March 5, 2005:
At St. John the Evangelist after Communion I could see a flying locust up close and how they were coming up out of the ground. Jesus said: *"My people, this vision of locusts is a sign that these hordes are going to continue to threaten food crops in various areas of the world. These disturbances will be one more step to the coming world famine as hunger will be spreading more, especially in the third world. In some places these disasters will be a punishment for sin and wars. The Gospel reading of the Pharisee and the tax collector in the Temple should focus your prayer more on seeking your forgiveness of your sins than lauding how good you are. I have created you as spirit and body, and I know that you are all good in yourselves, but you also need to admit that you are weak sinners in need of My grace. That is why the tax collector gained more out of his visit to the Temple because he was asking for My mercy. In the Old Testament the people sacrificed animals and crops, but you have the most Divine sacrifice of all in My death on the cross. At every sacrifice of the Mass, I am being offered up for your sins, so you do not have to make any sacrifices of animals. It is mercy that I desire you to seek instead of animal sacrifices. There are other sacrifices or penances that you can do during Lent to atone for your sins and help your spiritual life. Trust in Me that I will always be watching over you to protect your soul from the evil ones."*

Later, at St. Theodore's tabernacle I could see layers of ash and pumice all over the ground. I then saw dark clouds of ash and a volcano spewing out lava. The scene backed out and up so I could see the volcano coming from Yellowstone, and black covered much of the United States. Jesus said: *"My people, I have told you that I would bring America to its knees with major disasters. This volcanic disturbance is definitely from Yellowstone and it will create a massive effect on your crops and on your weather. Many in its path will be killed, but there will be increasing earthquakes before this eruption. It is not a matter of whether it will happen, but only when it will happen. You have seen larger and larger earthquakes with the latest tsunami. The earth is about to be shaken to its core as the poles will be in a state of flux. Those,* who could not believe that you are in the end times, will be humbled with more catastrophic events. Even the evil ones will be humbled by My smiting them of their power, especially with My comet of chastisement that will destroy the reign of the Antichrist. I have shown you before how the evil ones will be suffering a hell on earth as they suffer the flames that will not consume them. My faithful will be protected as I renew the earth in preparation for My Era of Peace. My justice will fall on the unjust, while My mercy will rest on My faithful remnant. Do not be fearful of these events for I will protect your souls from the evil ones. Call on My help and you will be saved."

Sunday, March 6, 2005:
At Holy Name after Communion I could see a train and I was looking ahead to follow the track. Jesus said: *"My people, a train track is like following your mission path to heaven. It has been laid out for you to follow ahead of time. You have free will to follow Me or not. When you refuse to follow Me, you many times are like the destruction of a derailment. The distractions of the world can lead you off on a side track detour and you will not be able to accomplish the mission that I have given you. Each of you has been given unique talents and skills to carry out your specific mission. Remember this also when you are contemplating abortions. Look at all of the skills being wasted by your frivolous killing of My little ones. If you keep on the right track in life, then you will be directed to eternal happiness with Me in heaven."*

Monday, March 7, 2005:
At Holy Name after Communion I could see someone hiding behind a building. Jesus said: *"My people, do not hide from your fears and from your hates of others by avoiding them. I want you to love everyone and it starts with being able to forgive everyone. You may have some in your family that in your mind may have violated you in some way. In order to have peace and harmony in your family, you must be willing to forgive any hurts between your relatives. Life is too short to hold grudges, or keep*

away from the ones you should love. Work to reach out and repair any hard feelings, even with those who may have addictions. Even if your relatives continue to refuse your overtures, keep giving them good example in your love. Even in the world it is hard to forgive killers, abortionists, and terrorists, but you are still called to pray for everyone and love them. Loving your enemies and forgiving them starts with loving Me and forgiving yourself of your sins. Frequent Confession can cleanse your souls so you have the power of My grace and love to share with others. Get your own spiritual house in order so you will not be a hypocrite in what you believe. Love and forgiveness should pervade all of your actions and you will be moving closer to that needed perfection to gain heaven."

Later, at St. Theodore's tabernacle I could see a dove flying in the air and there was a wolf pack chasing after me. Jesus said: *"My people, during the coming tribulation you will be traveling in the wilderness among many dangerous wild animals on your way to My refuges. Just as I will protect you from harm by the evil ones, I also will protect you from any wild animals. You are seeing the dove representing the Holy Spirit, and He will be your guardian of protection. You will see this protection at My refuges and on the way to your refuges. I will make it so the animals will not see you or smell you. I will even deliver some animals such as deer to you for meat. Your testing time will be coming soon when you will have to put your full trust in Me for protection, food, water, and shelter. When you call on My help in faith, everything will be miraculously provided for all of your needs. Even when things will seem hopeless, I will come with power to defeat the Antichrist and all the evil ones. So do not lose hope, but trust in My victorious power that will bring you into My Era of Peace with no fear."*

Tuesday, March 8, 2005:

At St. Theodore's Adoration I could see a swarm of black flies all over everything and people were being bitten up badly. Jesus said: *"My people, man has caused nature to become more unbalanced by all the mischief he has done with the plants and animals. You have experimented with bee production and you created killer bees. You have modified insecticides so many mutations of insects are creating plagues of locusts, grasshoppers, and other insects that eat your crops. Many of your cancers and diseases are a result of your bad methods of producing food and man-made diseases for population control. Man needs to go back to the ways that I have created things and stop upsetting the balance of nature as I created it. Nature is rebelling against man's abuses and you will be seeing worse storms and food famines all over the world as a result. I have warned you many times that your abuse of your environment will affect your lives in many ways that you did not realize in the effects on your delicate earthly balance. Strive to follow My ways in nature and not man's abuses and you will have fewer problems."*

Wednesday, March 9, 2005:

At St. John the Evangelist after Communion I could look out on some pews in a church from the side and there were fewer people coming to Mass. Jesus said: *"My people, do not be discouraged or disheartened when you see fewer people coming to Mass on Sunday and fewer people coming to your prayer groups. This will be a challenge in faith in the end times and many will fall away and turn their backs on Me. It is because of the spiritual laziness of people that I am taking away many blessings from America. Your affluence and earthly activities have taken the place of your worship of Me, and you are in effect worshiping the idols of money and possessions. I still will never forget you and I am always awaiting sinners to repent, but I will not force My love on you. My people need to come in prayer and worship Me at Mass if they wish to establish a loving relationship with Me. If you do not say, 'I love you,' to Me, how can I know that you are sincere when you call My Name? I have the words of eternal life, and if you refuse to follow My Will, then you will be walking the broad road to hell instead of the narrow road to heaven. Choose eternal life with Me, or you will suffer forever from the devil and the flames of hell."*

Later, at Holy Name I could see rays of bright light shine down from heaven. Among the rays of light I could see large double helixes representing strands of DNA. Jesus said: *"My people, when you were conceived, the strands of DNA in that first cell were the gift of your parents, but the soul that I joined with your body is My creation that gives you life. All of your physical traits, your eye color, whether you are right handed, the gift of your intelligence, and your skin color are all who you are, and are found in your DNA. You would not want to alter your DNA because it would change who you are. In the same way why would you want to alter the traits of plants and animals even by cloning? By man's manipulation of DNA, you are also changing the identity of a perfect plan that I had for that plant or animal. It is these changes that I abhor and nature will rebel against your mischief because man's manipulations do not take into account the balance of nature. It is one thing to research things to learn how life works, but it is entirely wrong to seek research just to change nature to man's idea of perfection. It is these changes that man needs to stop making before they create monsters that could destroy life instead of prolonging it. Be satisfied with My perfection in creation because anything man makes is imperfect and will upset nature's delicate balance."*

Thursday, March 10, 2005:
At St. John the Evangelist after Communion I could see a crack at the bottom of a closed door and light was shining through the bottom. Jesus said: *"My people, you are familiar with the image of Me knocking on the door of your heart to let Me in. It is everyone's free will to open this door to My graces which are the light shining through the bottom crack. To open the door it means that you are willing to accept Me as Lord in your life and that you will repent of your sins. Once you accept that you are a sinner and want My forgiveness of your sins, this is the first step. Then you become sorry for your sins in offending Me, and you are willing to take the next step to the confessional. At Confession you admit your sins to the priest and I absolve you from your sins through the priest's absolution. Now I have set you free of your sins and My light shines forth My graces into your heart as the door is*

opened. It is this constant openness to confess your sins that will keep your soul pure and keep a loving relationship with Me. I long to forgive the repentant sinner and welcome you back to My love. My graces and forgiveness are always available to you. All you have to do is make the forward step as the lepers who wanted to be cleansed. Keep the light of My grace always burning in your souls and you will be well on your way to heaven."

Later, at the prayer group at Holy Name Adoration I could see the bottom part of an ornate church with beautiful woodwork. Jesus said: *"My people, you are saddened today by the latest news of a priest being arrested for misuse of offensive pictures on the internet. You are living in an evil age and I have asked: 'Will I find any faithful at the end times?' Even though you are seeing disturbing things, I do not want you to despair in your sorrow. This only points out how much more that you need to pray for your priests. Remember that I am always with you to raise up your spirits when you are down and to give Me your burdens to help you carry them. Trust in My power that is greater than Satan and come to Me in Confession to release you of all of your sins, both large and small."*

I could see someone kneeling in prayer for a long time. Jesus said: *"My people, Lent is a time when prayer should be your main focus in answer to all the sin in your world. Prayer is needed for all of your secular and spiritual leaders, especially My pope son, John Paul II. Prayer is needed for all sinners because you have not reached your judgment yet. Prayer is needed for all the souls in purgatory. There are many needs for prayer and that is why it is so important to make time to pray. Pray with your heart so it is sincere and not just lip service. I listen to all of your prayers."*

I could see a fireplace with some wood next to it. Jesus said: *"My people, some use wood all the time to heat their houses in winter. Most use gas and oil to heat their homes because there is less maintenance. It is still appropriate to have a secondary source of heat in the cold. There are many causes of power outages and those who are prepared will have warm houses. You are all seeing energy prices of various fuels rise, so it is even more advantageous to use cheaper sources of fuel. These high prices are also teaching you good conservation by minimizing your fuel needs."*

I could see some tall columns of some government buildings as you are seeing problems with your deficits and higher local taxes. Jesus said: *"My people, your local governments are dealing with higher medical costs and increasing costs for retirement benefits for government employees. These tax increases are causing more burdens on those with fixed incomes that already are paying more for drugs, gasoline, and heating bills. You will be seeing heavier resistance by your taxpayers to take on higher taxes and higher deficits that increase taxes and devaluate your currency. Pray for your leaders to lessen your tax burden than increasing it when they spend irresponsibly."*

I could see some old guns and then some modern weapons. Jesus said: *"My people, your country is spending far too much money on weapons and supporting constant unnecessary wars. Your defense budget is one of the biggest expenditures, but it does not have to be that way if people were more reluctant to keep from entering more wars for whatever trumped up reasons being given. Your prayer efforts also need to be focused on peace in your world and not forcing democracy on nations at the end of a gun. Seek peace and harmony with your neighbors instead of finding reasons to go to war. Love will go farther than making nations angry with wars."*

I could see a large crematorium as a means to incinerate bodies. Jesus said: *"My people, in World War II you were abhorred at finding crematoriums in the death camps in Germany. In several places in your country such crematoriums have been made for ridding those who will not go along with the coming new world order. I have prepared you to be ready to leave for My refuges so you will be protected from the killing and the torture by the evil ones who will be coming to power for a short time. Pray much that you will be strong in these end times by calling on My grace."*

I could see some boats being tossed around in some heavy sea storms. Jesus said: *"My people, you must admit that your hurricanes and tornadoes are becoming more violent and more frequent causing more deaths and destruction than ever before.*

Some ascribe increasing temperatures in your global temperatures that are increasing this intensity. Others are showing manmade weather machines are affecting this increase. Still others speak of sunspot activity and effects from large events in your galaxy. I am pointing out also that My wrath is also falling upon places of constant sin and some of these weather disasters are chastisements for sin. Pray for your country and its people because the weight of your sins will bring you to your knees."

Friday, March 11, 2005:

At St. John the Evangelist after Communion I could see a spiraling staircase go up for many floors. Jesus said: *"My people, when you think of aspiring to be with Me in heaven, it seems like a dauntless task to achieve the perfection of a saint to enter heaven. Even though in man's eyes this may seem impossible, yet with Me all things are possible. Myself and My Blessed Mother are the only ones that did not sin. Even the saints sinned, but they were converted through My grace to be examples of goodness for all My faithful to imitate their lives. Take each day and walk with Me through all of your trials and temptations. I will not test you beyond your endurance. I will always give you enough grace to sustain you through everything that you will face in life. So do not let sin, fears, or anxieties disturb your peace, but be confident in Me and trust in My help. Before you start any task, call on My help first so I can relieve your burdens. Do not think that you can accomplish everything on your own. After you were frustrated in your feeble attempts to work through something, you finally come to pray for your intention. By asking Me first in prayer, you will see things in life will be a lot easier to bear. It is good to build up your spiritual confidence in My help, and you will minimize any of your worries because I will take care of them with your cooperation."*

Later, at St. Theodore's tabernacle I could see an empty wheelchair in a barn with some hay around. Jesus said: *"My people, I want you to pray for and help the infirm, the disabled, and those that are handicapped. These are some of the works of mercy that you can perform to store up treasures in heaven. The sick need your care to return them to good health. Those with chronic or permanent problems with backs and knees need help with wheelchairs and their physical needs. By the grace of God you may be healthy now, but some day you may have to deal with needing assistance to move around. If you have friends or relatives in need of your help, do not avoid any call for help, but assist them joyfully without question. Every person that you help, you are helping Me in them. The sick and disabled also appreciate your visits and your concern for their welfare. You will receive many graces for doing such good deeds. You have opportunities for graces every day, so do not commit any sins of omission by not reaching out to My sick and disabled souls."*

Saturday, March 12, 2005:
At St. John the Evangelist after Communion I could see an ugly beast and a green scale came off of his eyes and he opened his now black piercing eyes that I shied away from. Jesus said: *"My people, this vision of the beast opening his black piercing eyes is a sign to you that his coming into power is close. I have told you that I would be the one to free him for his brief reign that will be a test for all souls on the earth. Many are weak and are in the power of the evil one already. The general people do not realize that unless they have Me with them, they will not be able to be saved from the Antichrist. My Warning will be My gift of mercy for all souls to be prepared not to accept the mark of the beast and not to worship the Antichrist. So if the Antichrist is about to declare himself, then you know the time of the Warning is also close to happening. I have told you that the Warning will be heralding the beginning of the Antichrist's coming to power. Lent is a good time to prepare your soul for the coming evil onslaught when I will protect all souls who call on My help. Build up your spiritual strength now and have your blessed Benedictine crosses on your person to protect yourselves from the evil ones."*

Later, at St. Theodore's tabernacle I could see the map of the United States and it was aflame. Jesus said: *"My people of America, this map of the United States burning up in flames is the same fate as other great civilizations such as the Roman Empire. This old empire fell from within because of its loss of morals. America is repeating this destruction in the same way because of all of your immorality in abortions, fornication, adultery, and same-sex marriages. Do you not see the moral fiber of your country falling apart with all of the sex, violence, and foul language in your TV programming and movies? I tell you because of your sins and idol worship of money and possessions in place of Me, you will meet with My swift justice. Wars, deficits, natural disasters, and terrorism will bring your country down as chastisements for your sins. You have seen My justice in Noah's day and with Sodom and Gomorrah. So do not expect any fewer stripes for your sinful behavior. The just I will reward, but the unjust will face the fires of hell."*

Sunday, March 13, 2005:

At Holy Name after Communion I could see the Shroud of Turin with the top view on one side and the back view on the other side. Jesus said: *"My people, all of today's Gospel is focused on Me as the Resurrection and the Life. The vision is of My burial cloth. When I resurrected, My radiance of light burned My image into the cloth. The raising of Lazarus from the grave and his burial clothes are a foreshadowing of My own Resurrection on Easter Sunday. I asked Mary and Martha if they believed in the resurrection of the dead. This is a core belief in your faith because My Resurrection is also a foreshadowing of every soul that will continue to have life after death. My Transfiguration, that showed My glorified body in all of its brilliance, shows you how those, who are faithful, will also be reunited with their bodies in the glory of heaven. Without this hope of resurrection, you would not have much to live for, with no reward for following My ways. So rejoice now in this life for My victory over death and sin. I have paid the price for your sins and by accepting Me as your Savior, you will truly be saved and resurrected at the final judgment."*

Monday, March 14, 2005:
At Holy Name after Communion I could see a mandolin representing an instrument that Daniel may have used in his psalms. Jesus said: *"My people, the two elders, who were charged with perjury against Susanna by Daniel (Dan 13:1-63), shows that even your leaders can be corrupted. Many trust those in authority to tell the truth, but even your elected officials can be tainted by sexual offenses or financial rewards. Everything must be discerned against My Commandments to determine that it is true. There are also prophets in every age that are revealing the truth of many sins going on in your society. If the Holy Spirit did not alert Daniel to this injustice against Susanna, the elders could have had her killed, even though she was innocent. Even your justice system is warped with unjust laws that allow abortion, pornography, and same-sex marriages to continue unchallenged. The moral deterioration of your country is evident in what your society allows. Speak out against these unjust laws, or you will be condemned for condoning them with your silence."*

Later, at Our Lady of Lourdes Adoration I could see some small caves and some roots going into the ground. Jesus said: *"My people, these roots in the ground represent My faithful remnant that will always be well grounded in the faith, even when many have fallen away from Me. My faithful are about to witness a persecution all over the world that will be worse than they have ever seen. The evil ones will soon be coming into power, and you will need My protection with My Blessed Sacrament, your rosary, and your blessed Benedictine crosses. I am preparing My refuges of protection for when you will have to flee from your homes. When there is an artificial famine, a schism in My Church, and forced chips in the body, this will be the sign to call on Me and I will have My guardian angels lead you to My refuges for all of your needs. I will protect My Church from the evil ones and you will not be harmed at My refuges. Have trust and hope in My victory over evil, even when it may appear hopeless. Keep rooted in your faith in Me and you will have nothing to fear."*

Tuesday, March 15, 2005:

At Holy Name after Communion I could see lightning striking from a dark cloud as the darkness came over Jesus as He died on the cross. Jesus said: *"My people, when Moses raised the bronze serpent, all of those, who were bitten by the serpents, could live by looking on the bronze serpent. This is a strong connection to Me in the Gospel, since those, who look upon Me and follow My laws, will also live on in the Spirit as well. This is a foreshadowing of how I would be lifted up on the cross for all to see and be redeemed. The bronze serpent is also another foreshadowing of the luminous crosses that will be over My refuges. When you look on these luminous crosses, you also will be healed of all of your infirmities. I provided for people in healing in the Exodus and I will be providing healing during the coming modern day Exodus as well. Even today many healings come by calling on My Name and blessing people with My crucifix. I am the Great Healer of sicknesses both in the body and in the soul. Your most important healing can come in Confession as your sins are cleansed and your soul is healed in My grace."*

Later, at St. Theodore's Adoration I could see a lot of clocks all striking the hour and then they all disappeared and there was stone in their place. Jesus said: *"My people, you are here today and buried tomorrow. Your life here is short as you see the flowers wilt. In the beginning of your life time seemed very slow, but now in your later years the years are flying by like fence posts seen going by from a speeding car. This vision of the clocks suddenly disappearing means that the time for this age is drawing to a close. Even before you die in your physical body by normal aging, it is possible that I could bring an end to this life. Once you see the Antichrist come to power as he is declared, you will know My time of coming to defeat him is very close. You need to be spiritually prepared to meet Me at your judgment because you could die at any time. Even more so at the time of tribulation, your faith will be tried to its breaking point. Call on My help and I will be there to save you from the evil ones. At this time of trial I will have your angels lead you to My refuges of protection. With Me beside you, you will be saved. So do not fear how you will be tested. The Holy Spirit will give you what to say in your trials before men, so do not be afraid to witness My Good News, even when your life may be endangered."*

Wednesday, March 16, 2005:
At St. John the Evangelist after Communion I could see a farm with a little white house and a thatched roof. Jesus said: *"My people, I keep showing you signs of a simpler life because you spend your time on too many activities that will never help you to heaven. When you go around your house and clean up the clutter, you are free of things in your way. It is the same way in your spiritual life. You spend your time on many distractions, bad habits of addiction, and unnecessary busy tasks every day. By living a simpler life with less clutter in stealing your time, you would have more time for Me in prayer and for helping others. It all comes down to priorities. In your house you decide what is important to keep, and the rest you dispose of. In your spiritual life you decide what will help you to heaven and keep them, but those things that will not gain you heaven, you can dispose of also. This is why a simple life without rushing and without many distractions is better for your spiritual life. The more you can detach yourself from your sinful habits, addictions, and possessions, the closer you will be to the perfection that you need to enter heaven, and this will set you free as in the Gospel."*

Later, at St. Theodore's Adoration I could see a vision of someone's front yard from the side of the house. There were bushes around the perimeter and a tall crucifix standing in the ground before me. Jesus said: *"My people, it does not matter whether you live in the city, a suburb, or on a farm. I watch over you wherever you live and you are called to My service. The crucifix in the ground means that you are to give witness to My suffering on the cross in the example of your own suffering. Some have to bear sicknesses, or chronic health problems, or even deaths in the family. It is not easy in this life to carry your cross because you do not know what will happen to you next. If you have faith and trust in My help, you will have nothing to fear. Keep close to Me in your prayers and frequent Confession, and you will be* able to bear all the burdens of life. Rejoice in My graces and blessings because I will protect your soul from the evil ones."*

Thursday, March 17, 2005: (St. Patrick)
At St. John the Evangelist after Communion I could see a bunch of pencils wrapped with a rubber band and an exam room with many taking a test. Jesus said: *"My people, these students taking an exam are a representation of how every day everyone is faced with a test of being a Christian in their actions. At the judgment day you will be again walking through every day of your past life, and you will have to make an accounting of all of your actions each day as well as the intentions of your actions. I see every one of your actions and you do not fool Me with your outside actions because I know the intentions in your heart and what you are doing in secret. All of heaven and those around you also see your actions, so you should be mindful of giving good example in all that you do. Some people try to hide their sins in secret, but they are only fooling themselves and not Me. Many will feel great guilt for their sins when they see them in their life review. You can prepare for your death and your Warning experience by reflecting on your sins and confessing them to the priest in the confessional. You cannot change your sins, but they can be forgiven and you can start making reparation for your sins on earth instead of waiting to suffer more in purgatory. You can work to stop repeating your habitual sins, so you will have less to make reparation for. My death on the cross paid for your sins, so claim My graces by seeking My forgiveness."*

Later, at the prayer group at Holy Name Adoration I could see the entrance to the burial place of Jesus in the Holy Sepulcher Church in Jerusalem. Jesus said: *"My people, you have heard Me say many times that 'I am the Resurrection and the Life.' At every funeral that you attend, you know that this soul had to come to Me in judgment. No matter how much you might wish that this soul should go straight to heaven, it is proper that you pray for his soul in case he is found in purgatory. If they are not there, then your prayers will be directed to other souls in purgatory. If he is in purgatory, then he will thank you even more for *shortening his time there."*

I could see some green vestments and a casket as at an Irish wake. Jesus said: *"My people, I know many have a great love for St. Patrick and especially those of Irish descent. On his feast day many of the Irish people remember their dearly departed as they pray for his intercession for their souls if they are still in purgatory. You, yourself, have Irish ancestry, so it is special to remember your parents and all of your family members that have passed on. These souls are grateful for your remembering them."*

I could see a great white light and all the stars of the universe traveled around this light. Jesus said: *"My people, you look out on a clear night and are awed by the size and order of the universe of stars. I am the Second Person of your God who created all that you see in the heavens, and even all that you have not seen as well. Give praise and glory to your God for all of My creation and a special thanks that I have created you as well. Your very life is a gift of God given to each soul. Thank Me for all that I have done for you."*

I could see people dressing in green and even some shopkeepers were celebrating St. Patrick's Day. Jesus said: *"My people, there are those who commercialize certain feast days that traditions have honored for many years. Even Easter has people buying candy and making Easter eggs with bunnies. This may be well for the shopkeepers, but My faithful know there is a deeper meaning to My death on Good Friday and My Resurrection on Easter Sunday. You are about to conclude this Lenten Season with the coming Passion Week. Make yourself available to all these beautiful services that walk you along My path to Calvary. My death has given everyone an opportunity for salvation. My sacrifice of My Body and Blood has atoned for everyone's sins. Accept Me as your Savior and come to Me in Confession to forgive your sins."*

I could see someone cleaning their home in preparation for the family get together on Easter Sunday. Jesus said: *"My people, it is good for you to meet on the holy days because it unites your family with the Holy Family. As you come together in joy, you can share the gift of life that holds you all as one large family. As you celebrate My Resurrection, you are also celebrating your gift of spiritual life as well. It is your belief in My Resurrection that gives you hope one day of resurrecting your own body with your soul. This glorified body is the same body that I showed My apostles."*

I could see a thin sliver of light that fell on those poor souls that are existing in a comatose state. Jesus said: *"My people, your definitions of life in your laws and judgments make it hard to discern who should be kept alive and who should be allowed to die. My pope son has talked to you about how a person needs breathing and hydration. Feeding tubes and other means for life have been debated and you need to discern what is proper for your loved ones. Usually a person's health will dictate your response, but there is a time when heroic measures become futile. Pray and discern what is best for each person's welfare."*

I could see a vision of the Blessed Mother holding some flowers as at a funeral. Jesus said: *"My people, as you follow Me in My passion and death, think of how much My Blessed Mother had to suffer in watching her innocent Son beaten and crucified to please an angry mob. She knew of My mission and the prophecy of Simeon that she would suffer such sorrows. All the mothers, who have lost sons, should be comforted by My Blessed Mother because she is your mother also. My Blessed Mother even comes to help lead each soul to Me at their death. Those who have a deep love for My Blessed Mother in her rosary and her scapular will have My Blessed Mother intercede on their behalf to save their souls. Rejoice that you have such a heavenly intercessor at the time of your death."*

Friday, March 18, 2005:
At St. John the Evangelist after Communion I could see various insects and ants going about their tasks as God had directed them. Jesus said: *"My people, all of nature is ordered to My plan by instinct and survival. Man is made to My Image in that I gave you free will to love Me and follow My Will. You also have instincts for survival, but you also have reason to think and choose. I have a plan for every human being and I desire you to follow My Will. If you follow My Will, you will use your talents properly to achieve your mission in life. It is when you do not follow My laws that you fall into sin, and you will have difficulties in performing your mission in live. You are here to accomplish things for My glory and not any fame of your own. I am showing you*

this example of order in nature so that you can understand the harmony of following My ways over man's ways. You are made up of a physical and spiritual life in the body and the soul. By being in My grace through frequent Confession, you can walk in harmony with following My Will."

Later, at St. Theodore's tabernacle I could see a huge white comet tail come very close to the earth and many became frightened that it may even hit the earth. Jesus said: *"My people, I have told you that on the day of the Warning experience people would be frightened from what they saw in the sky. Now I am showing you a comet that will come close to the earth with a great white tail that will frighten many when they see this event. I have told you to be spiritually ready with pure souls for the Warning which is coming soon. This sign of a comet tells you that the Warning also is approaching soon. Everyone will see Me and you will have a life review of their good and bad actions. If you have serious sins on your soul, you could have a vision of yourself in hell. This will be a mercy for sinners and an opportunity for conversion from your habitual sins. My faithful will be working at a fever pitch to bring as many souls as possible back to Confession because of the guilt of their sins. Look for the signs of these events in the skies as the Warning will be the beginning of events leading up to the time of the Antichrist declaring himself."*

Saturday, March 19, 2005: (St. Joseph)
At St. John the Evangelist after Communion I could see two pieces of wood intertwined as they were joined together on the floor and some water ran over them. Jesus said: *"My people, I am showing you these pieces of wood joined together to represent a joining of your will with following My Divine Will, and the water of Baptism uniting us. You read in the first reading about My covenant with Abraham that I would make him a father of nations and his descendants would be as numerous as the stars. Again in the Gospel My Blessed Mother gave her fiat and I was conceived in her by the power of the Holy Spirit. St. Joseph also agreed to follow the word of the angel and took My Blessed Mother into*

his home as his wife, even though she was with child. You have so many examples to follow in giving your own free will over to following My plan for your life. Instead of acting out just your desires, pray for discernment if it is the right thing to do according to My laws. If you give everything over to Me in full consecration, then I can work through you to accomplish great things for My glory. By the Blessed Virgin Mary and St. Joseph working with Me, they were the instruments in helping Me to bring salvation to all of mankind. You will be witnessing to My Passion and death on the cross in Holy Week, so you can appreciate how much I love each one of you enough to die for you. I bring love into your lives for Me and when you are married to bring forth your own children. Follow My laws and you will be greatly rewarded in heaven."

Later, at St. Theodore's tabernacle I could see some army people under an arch of a building that led into a city. Jesus said: *"My people, it is time to ask why America is involved in constant wars that do not gain anything for your country. For the answer all you need to do is follow the money being spent on your current war in Iraq. Oil companies and weapons manufacturers are the ones getting rich on the available contracts. You saw how corrupt the oil for food program was and you can imagine the billions of dollars being misappropriated in your own government. It is the rich who control the spending and they profit from wars. The deficits that increase the national debt, that are caused by wars, put more taxpayer interest in the pockets of the central bankers who hold the loans. Once you see that the rich profit from wars, then you find the same people who make excuses to start these wars. Pray and search for peace instead of seeking out more nations to destroy. Love comes in living peacefully with your neighbors and not forcing them to live according to your ways."*

Sunday, March 20, 2005: (Passion/Palm Sunday)
At Holy Name after Communion I could see a cross standing in the dark and an orange ball of Light that represented the Spirit of Jesus leaving His Body. Jesus said: *"My people, I am showing*

you the Spirit of My Soul as it left My Body when I died on the cross. I became human with a mortal body and My Soul so I could offer My life up to My Father for the perfect sacrifice that would atone for all of mankind's sins. This separation of body and soul at death has been a consequence of Adam's original sin. When I was resurrected in a glorified body, I still had the five wounds in My Body which was a witness that it was the same body. With My Resurrection I give everyone hope after their death that they too can be resurrected with their glorified body after the final judgment. I also became the new Adam, so by Baptism in the Spirit, your original sin can be forgiven. Now with My sacraments you can be freed of your sins even while you are still alive on earth. Rejoice today as you lift your palms to My glory and My victory over sin and death."

Monday, March 21, 2005:

At Holy Name after Communion I could see printing presses turning out the daily newspaper. Jesus said: *"My people, I am showing you this newspaper being printed because My Good News of salvation is the most important news that you could receive about your eternal life. You have Bibles all over, but unless you pick one up and read it, My Word will not be read. The Good News is that I died for all of mankind's sins and you are now set free of your sins. This should be shouted from the rooftops to every soul that will listen. If you come to Me for forgiveness, I will cleanse your soul and grant you My grace to restore your soul to the purity after your Baptism. Do not pass up this opportunity to deny your sins and convert your life to worshiping Me instead of the idols of the world. Those, who love Me and follow My Will, are on the right path to heaven. Do not remain in bondage in the darkness of your sins, but come out into the beautiful light of My Easter celebration. By enduring your own Good Friday on earth, you will be carrying your cross to your own death, and then to your final reward in heaven. Be persistent and true to your faith in Me and you will have nothing to fear."*

Later, at St. Theodore's tabernacle I could see an atomic bomb experiment, a long blue microwave light going high up into the sky, and a brilliant blue light all along the horizon. Jesus said: *"My people, man, by all of his scientific madness, is threatening the very survival of everyone on the earth. Your nuclear proliferation among nations threatens nuclear war. Your microwave experiments are threatening your weather and worsening earthquakes and volcanoes all over the world. Your pollution still threatens your warming of the earth and all of your droughts that could cause a world famine. All of your DNA manipulations are threatening diseases and pestilence that you have never seen before. When I return to vanquish all evil on the earth, I will renew the earth as I created it because man has almost destroyed My creations on earth. The blue light all along the horizon is a picture of how I will replenish the earth to its former beauty. Rejoice at My coming because I will restore life to harmony both in the physical world and the spiritual world."*

Tuesday, March 22, 2005:
At Holy Name after Communion I could see some dust being cleaned up. Jesus said: *"My people, from dust you were created and unto dust you shall return. This was the theme of Ash Wednesday at the beginning of Lent, and soon you will be ending Lent with the Saturday Vigil of My Resurrection on Easter Sunday. Holy Week is the most moving spiritual event of the year. This is your core belief in My death and Resurrection. This walk to Calvary with Me represents your whole life's struggle. Each day you pick up your daily cross and witness to your faith in Me by your actions. Your birth is blessed with Baptism as you enter the Church, and you are blessed with the Anointing of the Sick as you leave this life. All of your actions are offered up to Me as your life is consecrated for My glory. Give glory and praise to God for My gift of My life so that all of you may have life in the Spirit, even after your death. The joy of My Resurrection is a promise to all of My faithful that you will also see Me in Paradise."*

Later, at St. Theodore's Adoration I could see a monstrance with the Host and it was struck by a rock that broke the glass holding the Host. Jesus said: *"My people, in many ways sinners strike*

Me with their sins in offending Me. During My Passion I was struck in speaking the truth to the High Priest. I was struck many times in My scourging at the pillar. Then I was lanced with a spear on the cross. I suffered people spitting on Me and belittling My Divinity as the Son of God. I forgave these people for not knowing what they were doing. Even when you commit sins against Me, it is as if you were striking Me again at the pillar. You should be sorry for offending Me and be willing to confess your sins in Confession. With contrite hearts and repentance for your sins, I will pardon you and restore grace to your souls. Give Me reverence in My Blessed Sacrament and protect My consecrated Host from destruction and irreverence."

Wednesday, March 23, 2005:

At St. John the Evangelist after Communion I could see a reliquary holding a Blood sample of Jesus in Brugge, Belgium and later a snake hissing that represented the devil. Jesus said: *"My people, you are seeing this relic of My Blood because it is by the sacrifice of My Blood that your sins are washed clean from your soul. During My scourging and crucifixion it was the loss of My Blood that brought on My death. Even when the spear pierced My side, you saw blood and water come forth to indicate that I had given up My Blood for all of mankind's sins. You are about to go through these readings of My Passion and commemorate My death on Good Friday. Fridays and the three o'clock hour remind you of My death when you pray the Divine Mercy Chaplet. Remember that the devil is still among you and tempting you to sin. You must be on your guard to ask My help in fending off his temptations so you can keep your soul clean. Even if you should fall victim to sin, you can be cleansed again by seeking My forgiveness in Confession. My mercy awaits all repentant sinners, so do not remain in your sin, but go to the priest and I will release you of your spiritual burdens. I died for your sins, but if you do not seek My forgiveness, then My death was in vain for you. You have the opportunity in Confession to be freed of your sins, so take advantage of My gift of mercy and grace, and do not pass it by in your spiritual laziness."*

Later, at St. Theodore's Adoration I could see someone open a metal hatch on a warship and only darkness could be seen inside. Jesus said: *"My people, this hatch to a ship opened to darkness because this is how you went blindly into this war in Iraq. You have destroyed Saddam Hussein's tanks and armor, but you are bogged down in dealing with insurgent suicide attacks. It has become harder to exit without some means of authority present to keep order among the Iraqi people. The darkness inside the door is the unknown of how soon America will be able to leave these countries that it has invaded. Fighting a constant battle in a foreign land is not going to be popular with your people when your lost soldiers and expenses are not improving the situation. It would be better if you did not even start these wars because your exit strategy is too hard to determine. War is not going to gain America anything in this region. It would be better to leave gradually and stop interfering in these governments. It is love I desire of your people, but you cannot love your neighbor with constant wars. Look to live in peace without forcing your ways on these people."*

Thursday, March 24, 2005: (Holy Thursday)
At Holy Name after Communion I could see a cross and an orange ball of light rose into the sky and disappeared. Jesus said: *"My people, this ball of light represents My soul as I left the cross. On Holy Thursday I instituted My Holy Eucharist for every time you remember Me in the breaking of the bread at Mass. This life that left My Body is now present in every consecrated Host. I have not only died for each of you, I have given you Myself as captive in My Blessed Sacrament. I call on My faithful to give reverence to My Real Presence in My Eucharist and to receive Me without any mortal sin on their souls. Anyone who receives Me in mortal sin will receive no grace and will commit another sin of sacrilege. If you have mortal sin on your soul, you must confess it in Confession in order to receive My Eucharist worthily. You can adore Me at Adoration or in My tabernacle. You can show your love for Me by making special visits to My Blessed Sacrament. Every time you take time to be in My Presence, you will gain*

extra graces as your reward for your reverence and love."

Friday, March 25, 2005: (Good Friday)

At Holy Name after Communion I could see Jesus on the cross and I could focus in on all five wounds of Christ one at a time. Jesus said: *"My people, I am showing you each of My wounds so you could appreciate all that I went through in My Passion and death on the cross for your sins. Just as you commemorate My death, I am still suffering for all of those dying now from abortions, wars, killings, and from natural causes. When you die, you are brought before Me in your judgment when you will see all of your life before you. After you will see all of your sins and good deeds, you will agree that My judgment will be fair. Pray for the souls who are dying now, even as they share their suffering with My death. Everything that you have focused on in life leads up to this final moment of your death. When you have some quiet moments with Me, you can meditate how to prepare yourself spiritually so you are ready with a pure soul to meet Me at your death."*

Saturday, March 26, 2005: (Vigil of Easter)
At Holy Name I could see Jesus standing between two angels that were holding candles and I could still see His wounds in His hands. Jesus said: *"My people, I first appeared to the women at the tomb who came to put spices on My Body. They saw My glorified Body and they did not recognize Me until I called Mary by her name. As you read in the Gospel, I told the women to tell My disciples that I had risen from the dead as I told them that I would rise on the third day. My disciples had a hard time understanding what rising from the dead meant, so they found it hard to believe the women's report. Only when they saw the empty tomb for themselves did they believe. Still St. Thomas had to place his finger in My hands and My side to believe. I told My disciples: 'Blessed are they who believe in My Resurrection and have not seen Me as they did.' This is true of all of My faithful who have received My Good News and believe. I love all of you as evidenced in My gift of My life on the cross. I want all of you to love Me also and show your love in your prayers and your good deeds for others. My Resurrection is My ultimate victory over sin and death. It is also My promise to all the faithful who believe in Me that one day they also will be resurrected with a glorified body. Live your*

consecration so you can be with Me for all eternity in heaven."

Sunday, March 27, 2005: (Easter Sunday)
At Holy Name after Communion I could see Jesus walking out of the darkness and into a bright light. Jesus said: *"My people, when you see Me walk out of the darkness into the light, you are seeing all of the sins that I took on from all of mankind. My Father saw Me as sin and accepted My sacrifice on the cross as worthy atonement for all of mankind's sins. God the Father forgave the sin and the Holy Spirit restored life into My Body. The Light of My Resurrection blinded the soldiers guarding the tomb, but they were paid not to reveal what they saw. My disciples believed in My Resurrection when they saw the empty tomb and My wrappings folded neatly. I revealed Myself several times to My dis-*

ciples and they saw Me eat food and realized My Body was real and not a ghost. My disciples rejoiced that they could share this Good News with the rest of the world. They even were joyous that they were whipped for witnessing to the beliefs that I taught them. My disciples of today should also be joyful in proclaiming My Good News to all the nations."

Monday, March 28, 2005:
At Holy Name after Communion I could see a blackboard as at a school setting. Jesus said: *"My people, this blackboard is a teaching tool and I want to explain to you what rising from the dead means. You all are knowledgeable that death is a separation of the soul and the body. Everyone is also appointed to die, but death is also the only threshold to reach heaven. The apostles had seen Me raise Lazarus from the dead, but they could not comprehend anyone raising himself from the dead. They also had a hard time understanding My Divinity and that death could have no power over God. My plan of salvation of offering My life as a sacrifice for everyone's sins was also difficult to understand. The enlightening of the Holy Spirit helped to inspire the Gospel writers and infused this knowledge in My disciples so they could teach My Good News to all the nations. In today's Gospel the Jewish leaders tried to keep My Resurrection a secret by paying the soldiers to testify against it. But My appearances in bodily form to My disciples is evidence to everyone that I did rise from the dead on the third day as I foretold many times while I was alive. My disciples recognized Me only when I called their name and broke bread with them. At death you will also have your soul separated from your body, but you have hope in My Resurrection that at the final judgment your body will also be resurrected."*

Later, at Our Lady of Lourdes Adoration I could see an old tabernacle in a quiet church. Jesus said: *"My people, I have given Myself to you in My Blessed Sacrament in every tabernacle all over the world. You are to follow Me in My tabernacle until your dying day. In other words I have given you My example in My suffering to imitate Me and stay close to Me. You can stay close to Me in daily prayer, frequent Confession, and as many visits to*

My Blessed Sacrament that you can make. When you find yourself in front of My Blessed Sacrament, you have your Lord and Master always before you. Listen to My calling of My love for your souls and unite your heart and soul with Me in your daily consecration. You have witnessed great things in Holy Week as I died for you and rose again. I gave you Myself in the Last Supper when I instituted My Eucharist in the consecrated bread and wine. Always keep grasping to have your soul in Divine obedience to My Will by giving Me praise and glory for all I have done for you. Give Me thanks for My gift of My Eucharist to all of you. Even if only a few come to worship Me in Adoration of My Blessed Sacrament, these few are accepting My graces to be shared by the rest of My faithful. Come to Me with your petitions before My tabernacles and I will hear your prayers more closely for those who are close to Me in My Blessed Sacrament. Encourage others and especially those in your families to make frequent visits to Me in My tabernacles."

Tuesday, March 29, 2005:
At St. John the Evangelist after Communion I saw fissures and collapsing tunnels along the plate lines of the recent earthquakes. Jesus said: *"My people, these plates underground in the Indian Ocean are becoming more unstable with each major earthquake. Gradually, there will be a change in the landscape of this area. This pressure will continue to spread along related plate lines in the rest of the world as earthquake activity is increasing in intensity and frequency. This increased earthquake activity will also affect volcanic activity as well. Natural disasters are increasing with ever increasing amounts of deaths. All of these events are adding more signs of the coming tribulation described in the Scriptures. It is a time to prepare spiritually by seeking My forgiveness and for people to move away from these active earthquake sites that will only worsen with increased activity."*

Later, at St. Theodore's Adoration I could see some trees in a deserted spot in the woods. Jesus said: *"My people, various people have received messages or apparitions in the mountains, before springs and in churches. It is appropriate that those, who re-*

ceive messages from Me, should receive them before My Blessed Sacrament or during Holy Communion. Each message should be tested in the Spirit for its source and discerned with the Holy Spirit for the truth of its content. These messages are given to strengthen and assist the faithful in carrying out their Christian responsibilities, but they do not add to the revealed Word of the Scriptures. Heaven sends prophets and messengers of My Word to every age and every people. It is up to the faithful in prayer to test the words if they are in keeping with Scripture and the laws of God. If a message is true, it will also bear good fruit. Follow the words of the true messengers of God because I am directing My Word to you through them. I have told you many times that you are living in an evil age, and you are in great need of prayer and fasting for the souls living now. By your good example and prayer, you can bring many souls to conversion. Give glory to Me for all of those souls that you could bring to conversion. Give thanks for these messages, and put them into action to save souls."

Wednesday, March 30, 2005:

At Holy Name after Communion I could see Jesus walking up the stairs to an upper room to have supper with his disciples. Jesus said: *"My people, the Gospel of My meeting My disciples on the road to Emmaus is another example of how people had difficulty recognizing Me in My glorified body. I used that opportunity to explain the Scripture passages describing the coming Messiah, and the suffering servant of God. I showed them why I had to suffer and die to atone for all of mankind's sins, and to bring everyone salvation by My redemption. This is a fulfillment of God's promise to open the gates of heaven that were closed by Adam's sin. This breaking of bread in an upper room allowed My disciples to recognize Me and realize that I truly had risen. I vanished from their sight, but they clearly saw that I was flesh and blood in their midst eating with them. My explanations to them helped them to understand My Divinity and My plan for man's salvation. Many are touched by this account of how the hearts of the disciples were burning with desire to hear Me explain the Scriptures. Give glory and praise to God that you can recognize Me also in the breaking of the consecrated bread at Holy Communion time in every Mass."*

Later, at St. Theodore's Adoration I could see an outside scene and among some water and land I could see everything turn upside down in a massive earthquake. Jesus said: *"My people, you have seen two major earthquakes in close proximity within just three months. This vision of another massive earthquake with many deaths is how many major disasters are happening with a high intensity and in a shorter time between them. Before you have cleaned up one disaster, another is striking. You saw this also when four hurricanes struck Florida in one season. Many of these events are the worst ever or since many years ago. Natural disasters are occurring all over the world, but many are occurring near water. Open your eyes, My faithful, because I told you that you would see one major event following another. These signs of the end times should alert My faithful to get their spiritual lives in order because the tribulation is close. By having a pure soul from Confession, you will be ready to face Me in your Warning experience. Establish your love relationship with Me now while you can, since time for repenting will become more difficult as the Antichrist comes to power."*

Thursday, March 31, 2005:
At the prayer group at Holy Name Adoration I could see a lot of seats for a funeral, but there were only a few people without a casket. Jesus said: *"My people, your country has been drawn into a life and death issue over Terry Schiavo and it has polarized your culture of death with those who strive for life. Your laws have allowed the spouse to withdraw water and feeding tubes from a viable woman who had been living this way for fifteen years. Even My pope son favored the feeding. It is your doctors and judges that are determining who should die and who should live. There is a strong concern about euthanasia or mercy killing based on a certain quality of life. This case may be used to emphasize health proxies, but do not be quick to snuff out life early because you may be denying someone's suffering for the reparation of their sins."*

I could see a meeting of cardinals trying to decide how the Church should be run while the pope is too ill to act properly. Jesus said: *"My people, I want you to pray for the health of My pope son because he may be in his last days. It is difficult for the Church to have strong leadership while My pope son has a hard time communicating. Yet he is still pope until his death. These decisions about life and death may be coming in My pope son's position as well. Pray that your cardinals and bishops will provide the right leadership to direct My Church."*

I could see some people meeting to discuss government matters. Jesus said: *"My people, you are seeing many disagreements between various nations, ethnic groups, religious groups, and even among family members. Instead of wanting to fight each other, I desire that you all love God and your neighbor. This is My Law of love that binds everyone in harmony, instead of discord and wars. This even means that I am calling you to love your enemies, whether they are abortionists, or Islamic terrorists. This is a hard challenge, but love will heal more hurts than constant wars that solve nothing."*

I could see some election booths being taken down. Jesus said: *"My people, your last election voiced many opinions on many subjects and it created many divisions. The most important issue focused on moral issues and family values. After all the talk, America made amends and healed some of its differences. So after many of these court cases on death, it is time to make peace among your people and not accentuate your divisions. If you truly want to follow My laws, then love one another."*

I could see a beautiful rich building with fancy foods and people outside were trying to break in. Jesus said: *"My people, you have seen struggles with your homeland security and more recently troubles with Mexican people trying to cross into America for your jobs and health services. You have one side exploiting these foreigners for cheap labor and you have the current residents who are having their jobs and taxes threatened to support these illegal immigrants. Security has been a problem, especially since the terrorists took down your buildings. Unfortunately, this striving to fight a war on terrorism has left you with constant wars with no way out, and a striving for a National Identification through smart cards in your driver's licenses. Be aware how so-called noble causes are being used to take away your rights. Strive for laws that are fair to everyone and not just the rich."*

I could see some people driving cars, a few people using horses, and others experimenting with other technologies for transportation. Jesus said: *"My people, your ease of transportation has been taken for granted for many years in your use of gasoline cars. Now with high prices for oil and gasoline, people are starting to seriously consider alternate fuels and alternate means of transportation. Ways that do not affect your environment are one incentive, and fuels other than oil could change your political landscape. Work to help each other instead of wasting energy and using energy to control people."*

I could see people praying the Divine Mercy Chaplet. Jesus said: *"My people, you are in your Divine Mercy Novena preparing for Mercy Sunday where you can have the reparation due for your sins forgiven with My mercy. Celebrating My Easter victory over sin and death carries over into My forgiveness of your sins. Each person has to make a free will decision to choose to follow Me and accept Me as his Savior and Redeemer. I will have mercy in My forgiveness on all repentant sinners, but you must make the first step to admit that you are sinners, and are in need of My grace of forgiveness in Confession. Rejoice in My mercy as you are rejoicing in My Resurrection."*

Index

abortion anniversary proper burial for infants (Jesus)	1/22/2005
abortion descriptions hard to avoid loss of life (Jesus)	1/22/2005
abortion punishment America will pay (Jesus)	1/26/2005
abortions a consequence of sin (Jesus)	3/3/2005
abortions speak out against (Jesus)	2/4/2005
abortions in America to bring US to its knees (Jesus)	1/22/2005
Adam, new Jesus unblemished Lamb (Jesus)	2/2/2005
Adoration encouraged by pope (Jesus)	2/19/2005
Adoration needed for atonement of sin (Jesus)	1/27/2005
Adorers of Eucharist receive graces for all (Jesus)	3/28/2005
almsgiving rewarded in heaven (Jesus)	1/8/2005
America falling as Roman Empire did (Jesus)	3/12/2005
America fist of God striking (Jesus)	2/21/2005
America no gain in Iraq war (Jesus)	3/23/2005
America not enough prayer to save (Jesus)	2/21/2005
America wake up from sins (Jesus)	1/12/2005
America drained in money & military (Jesus)	2/11/2005
American immorality cause of chastisements (Jesus)	2/2/2005
America's sins path to destruction (Jesus)	2/21/2005
Antichrist brief reign is soon (Jesus)	3/12/2005
Antichrist defeated when in power (Jesus)	3/15/2005
Antichrist destroyed by comet (Jesus)	3/5/2005
Antichrist coming prepare soul while time (Jesus)	3/30/2005
Antichrist in stadiums avoid eyes on TV, pictures (Jesus)	1/15/2005
arms dealers profit from wars (Jesus)	1/1/2005
atomic attack could bring WWIII (Jesus)	1/25/2005
backbone of faith to speak out (Jesus)	1/17/2005
balance of nature is being destroyed (Jesus)	3/8/2005
Baptism takes away original sin (Jesus)	1/8/2005
Baptism & Confirmation free you from sins (Jesus)	2/2/2005
beacon of faith share faith & love (Jesus)	2/6/2005
beacons of light to share faith with others (Jesus)	1/19/2005
belief in Jesus with empty tomb (Jesus)	3/26/2005
Benedictine Crosses protection from demons (Jesus)	3/12/2005
Bible study helps growth in faith (Jesus)	2/17/2005
bind sins to foot of cross (Jesus)	2/9/2005
Blessed Mother in rosary & scapular (Jesus)	3/17/2005
Blessed Sacrament communicates God's love (Jesus)	2/25/2005
Blessed Sacrament attacks on Adoration & tabernacles (Jesus)	2/4/2005
boast in God not yourself (Jesus)	2/12/2005
body vs. soul struggle for perfection (Jesus)	2/1/2005
breaking of bread repeated at Holy Communion (Jesus)	3/30/2005
Bush-State of Union war, abortion issues (Jesus)	2/2/2005
Calvary represents life's trials (Jesus)	3/22/2005
cars search for alternate fuels (Jesus)	3/31/2005
caves for protection (Jesus)	3/4/2005
caves as refuges for protection in tribulation (Jesus)	1/31/2005
central bankers hold the loans (Jesus)	3/19/2005
chastisements in areas of great sin (Jesus)	1/10/2005
chastisements in areas of sin (Jesus)	3/10/2005
child-like trust in God needed (Jesus)	2/12/2005
children protect from abuse (Jesus)	3/3/2005
children teach Real Presence (Jesus)	2/25/2005
chips in body time for going to refuge (Jesus)	2/10/2005
Christian life seen by your actions (Jesus)	1/25/2005
Christian witness by your good example (Jesus)	2/5/2005
cities protection underground (Jesus)	3/4/2005
clocks should not run your life (Jesus)	2/18/2005
cold hearts need warmth of God's love (Jesus)	1/21/2005
comet on day of Warning (Jesus)	3/18/2005
comet to destroy Antichrist's reign (Jesus)	3/5/2005
comet experiments could alter course to earth (Jesus)	1/20/2005
complaints of trials avoid to gain perfection (Jesus)	2/26/2005
computer technology being exported (Jesus)	2/17/2005
computer viruses to steal identities (Jesus)	1/14/2005
Confession best source of healing (Jesus)	3/15/2005
Confession making peace with God (Jesus)	2/26/2005
Confession mercy awaits all (Jesus)	3/23/2005
Confession repent of sins (Jesus)	3/22/2005
Confession restores spiritual power (Jesus)	2/17/2005
Confession sets us free of sins (Jesus)	3/10/2005
Confession souls pure, dirty like snow (Jesus)	1/7/2005
Confession curtain choice of forgiveness (Jesus)	1/17/2005
Confession needed to cleanse filth of sin (Jesus)	2/3/2005
Confession, frequent way to pure soul (Jesus)	1/24/2005
confidence in God better than our ways (Jesus)	2/18/2005
conscience, formed know right from wrong (Jesus)	2/26/2005
consecration focus on heavenly things (Jesus)	2/8/2005
consecration give all to Jesus (Jesus)	3/19/2005
conversion requirement personal commitment to Jesus (Jesus)	1/25/2005
conversions come through prayers (Jesus)	2/1/2005

Prepare for the Great Tribulation and the Era of Peace

Entry	Date	Entry	Date
Co-redemptrix with Jesus (Blessed Mother)	2/14/2005	endurance in life physical & spiritual tests (Jesus)	1/21/2005
creation gifts of God (Jesus)	2/7/2005	enemies love & forgive (Jesus)	3/7/2005
creation thank God for all (Jesus)	3/17/2005	eternal rest goal of earthly striving (Jesus)	1/28/2005
crematoriums for opposing new world order (Jesus)	3/10/2005	Eucharist gift of Jesus (Jesus)	3/24/2005
cross of Jesus example to carry our cross (Jesus)	1/31/2005	Eucharist gift of Jesus (Jesus)	2/7/2005
crosses of life (Jesus)	3/16/2005	euthanasia Terry Schiavo (Jesus)	3/31/2005
crosses in life accept like Jesus (Jesus)	1/2/2005	evangelists called to wake people up (Jesus)	1/5/2005
crucifix on altar shows Jesus' suffering (Jesus)	1/18/2005	evangelists,all called to save souls (Jesus)	1/23/2005
crucifix, holy pictures in every room of home (Jesus)	2/17/2005	evil age to come worse than ever seen (Jesus)	2/27/2005
culture of death hide abortion in language (Jesus)	1/26/2005	Exodus yesterday and today (Jesus)	3/15/2005
daily cross,pick up to follow Jesus (Jesus)	2/26/2005	faith build with daily prayer (Jesus)	3/3/2005
Daniel and Susanna (Jesus)	3/14/2005	faith in good & bad times (Jesus)	1/6/2005
David, my son personal message (David)	1/11/2005	faith stay rooted in (Jesus)	3/14/2005
death of Jesus share with dying people (Jesus)	3/25/2005	fast living slow down to see Jesus (Jesus)	1/18/2005
death, prepare for before your judgment (Jesus)	3/25/2005	fear is useless trust in God for needs (Jesus)	1/29/2005
debts increasing causing worse finances (Jesus)	1/27/2005	feeding tubes discerning life (Jesus)	3/17/2005
deer meat provided at refuges (Jesus)	3/7/2005	financial problems result of sin & greed (Jesus)	1/13/2005
deficits & wars need to be stopped (Jesus)	2/11/2005	food preparation can cause disease to spread (Jesus)	1/20/2005
detention center martial law is close (Jesus)	2/10/2005	forgiveness and sacrifice of cross (Jesus)	3/5/2005
detention centers trains carry captured to (Jesus)	2/19/2005	forgiveness from God & to others (Jesus)	1/27/2005
devil tests us with worldly desires (Jesus)	1/15/2005	forgiveness in families (Jesus)	3/7/2005
disaster victims help with donations (Jesus)	1/6/2005	gift of life praise God for (Jesus)	3/22/2005
disaster's cause natural order,punishment (Jesus)	1/4/2005	gifts & talents to heal & evangelize (Jesus)	1/6/2005
disasters, natural chastisements for sins (Jesus)	1/20/2005	God's agenda better than ours (Jesus)	2/14/2005
Divine Child & infancy honor all year (Jesus)	1/6/2005	Good News Holy Spirit inspired teaching of (Jesus)	3/28/2005
Divine Mercy Chaplet at 3:00 p.m. (Jesus)	3/23/2005	Good News share with all nations (Jesus)	3/27/2005
Divine Mercy Novena remission of reparation for sin (Jesus)	3/31/2005	Good News shout from the rooftops (Jesus)	3/21/2005
Divine obedience needed to follow God's Will (Jesus)	4/28/2005	Gospa House pleases Our Lady,4th anniv (Blessed Mother)	2/24/2005
Divine Will follow our mission (Jesus)	3/18/2005	grace sufficient for life (Jesus)	3/11/2005
Divine Will united to our will (Jesus)	3/19/2005	greed & war cause financial problems (Jesus)	1/27/2005
divisions need for healing (Jesus)	3/31/2005	HAARP machine makes weather worse (Jesus)	1/11/2005
DNA do not manipulate (Jesus)	3/9/2005	healings to come to this place (Jesus)	2/28/2005
DNA manipulation of (Jesus)	3/21/2005	heavenly treasure more valuable than money (Jesus)	2/11/2005
DNA research seek God's perfection (Jesus)	3/9/2005	high oil cost threatens fuel supply (Jesus)	2/15/2005
donations give to reputable groups (Jesus)	1/10/2005	Holy Family imitate a simple life (Jesus)	3/3/2005
earthquake activity higher with more deaths (Jesus)	3/29/2005	Holy Spirit protection at refuges (Jesus)	3/7/2005
earthquakes continuing with major deaths to come (Jesus)	3/30/2005	Holy Spirit at refuge protection against demons (Jesus)	2/8/2005
earthquakes,volcanoes by microwaves (Jesus)	3/21/2005	Holy Week most important of year (Jesus)	3/22/2005
Easter remember true meaning (Jesus)	3/17/2005	homosexual marriages speak out against (Jesus)	2/4/2005
Eastern Rite more reverence than Catholics (Jesus)	1/14/2005	humanity of unborn not debatable (Jesus)	1/22/2005
election of actions between good & evil (Jesus)	1/17/2005	hurts, let go stop grudges (Jesus)	1/27/2005
Emmaus, road to Scriptures explained (Jesus)	3/30/2005	idol worship in place of God (Jesus)	2/27/2005
end of age separate goats from lambs (Jesus)	3/3/2005	illegal immigrants National ID chips in licences (Jesus)	3/31/2005

Volume XXXVII

Imitation of Jesus reflected in your actions (Jesus)	2/4/2005	marriage needs loving communication (Jesus)	1/13/2005
immorality downfall of America (Jesus)	3/12/2005	masons in Church removing statues, tabernacles (Jesus)	1/14/2005
Indian Ocean earthquake plates still unstable (Jesus)	3/29/2005	messages, visions need testing in Spirit (Jesus)	3/29/2005
Iraq war leaving now a problem (Jesus)	3/23/2005	microwaves in weather & earthquakes (Jesus)	3/21/2005
Iraqi leader will be a militant on exit (Jesus)	1/1/2005	Middle East fighting over land, oil (Jesus)	2/16/2005
Iraqi war democracy difficult (Jesus)	1/1/2005	miracles of Eucharist prove Real Presence to doubters (Jesus)	
Jesus ask before doing anything (Jesus)	3/11/2005		2/25/2005
job loss gain for the rich (Jesus)	1/13/2005	mission in life path to heaven (Jesus)	3/6/2005
jobs lost,deaths challenges in life (Jesus)	2/18/2005	mission, unique each given unique gifts (Jesus)	1/13/2005
jobs, manufacturing lost to overseas (Jesus)	1/13/2005	mortal sin requires grace in living water (Jesus)	1/28/2005
judgement account for every minute (Jesus)	3/17/2005	mortal sins death to the soul (Jesus)	1/3/2005
justice of God overwhelmed by too much sin (Jesus)	2/21/2005	Moses lifted bronze serpent (Jesus)	3/15/2005
killing in wars unnecessary fo US (Jesus)	1/29/2005	mothers have no rights to kill infants (Jesus)	1/22/2005
Kingdom of God present in Jesus (Jesus)	1/13/2005	mountain top joy protection of Jesus (Jesus)	1/30/2005
ladder to heaven life's trials (Jesus)	2/1/2005	National ID chips in licences coming (Jesus)	3/31/2005
leaders also corrupted (Jesus)	3/14/2005	natural disasters one after another in end times (Jesus)	3/30/2005
Leary, Ray needs prayers (Jesus)	2/16/2005	natural disasters wherever you live (Jesus)	1/27/2005
Lent improve spiritual life (Jesus)	3/3/2005	nature rebelling for abuse of nature (Jesus)	3/8/2005
Lenten intentions prepare for now (Jesus)	1/6/2005	New Age idols remove from church (Jesus)	1/14/2005
Lenten penances plan for (Jesus)	1/27/2005	New Age songs avoid in church (Jesus)	1/20/2005
life's choices to heaven or hell (Jesus)	3/9/2005	new world order crematoriums prepared (Jesus)	3/10/2005
life's ups & downs tested by trials (Jesus)	1/30/2005	nuclear terrorism more potential from theft (Jesus)	1/25/2005
lifestyles of evil,divorce,abortion,gays (Jesus)	1/9/2005	oil & gasoline shortages could change lifestyles (Jesus)	2/15/2005
Light of Jesus direction for life (Jesus)	1/19/2005	one world control control buying & selling (Jesus)	1/14/2005
Light,salt of earth be witness of faith (Jesus)	2/5/2005	one world people cause of wars (Jesus)	2/21/2005
Living Water grace from sacraments (Jesus)	1/28/2005	one world people fear patriots & religious people (Jesus)	1/27/2005
locusts threaten food crops (Jesus)	3/5/2005	open mind to God needed for change (Jesus)	2/5/2005
love greatest message of Jesus (Jesus)	1/24/2005	openness needed for Divine Love (Jesus)	2/27/2005
love harmony of life & time (Jesus)	3/4/2005	original sin death a consequence (Jesus)	3/20/2005
love & happiness improves our lives (Jesus)	1/3/2005	original sin removed by Baptism (Jesus)	1/8/2005
love needed to gain heaven (Jesus)	1/13/2005	Our Lady of Lourdes Immaculate Conception (Blessed Mother)	
love of God better than fear of punishment (Jesus)	1/5/2005		2/14/2005
love of God create burning hearts of love (Jesus)	1/21/2005	patent protection not honored overseas (Jesus)	2/17/2005
Love of God in gift of life (Jesus)	2/25/2005	peace & love needed in your lives (Jesus)	2/5/2005
love of God teach others by actions (Jesus)	1/20/2005	peace found only in God (Jesus)	2/27/2005
love your enemies heal divisions (Jesus)	3/31/2005	peace in world starts with individual love (Jesus)	2/4/2005
love, words of need for God & neighbor (Jesus)	2/13/2005	peace, true with God's intervention (Jesus)	2/16/2005
Luminous Cross, Ca. third anniversary (Jesus)	2/9/2005	perfection for heaven with fasting & prayer (Jesus)	1/24/2005
Luminous Cross, Ca. three crosses for Trinity (Jesus)	2/28/2005	persecution speak out about faith (Jesus)	2/3/2005
luminous crosses over refuges (Jesus)	3/15/2005	Pope teaching authority of Church (Jesus)	2/22/2005
manufacturing jobs lost to cheap labor (Jesus)	2/17/2005	pope dying pray for good leadership (Jesus)	3/31/2005
Marie Esperanza present to family, guests Blessed Mother"	2/24/2005	Pope John Paul II being protected (Jesus)	2/19/2005
mark of beast shown in Warning (Jesus)	1/6/2005	Pope John Paul II hope for faithful (Jesus)	2/17/2005

Prepare for the Great Tribulation and the Era of Peace

pornography misused by priests (Jesus)	3/10/2005	Resurrection promise of our resurrection (Jesus)	3/26/2005
possessions hard to leave, control (Jesus)	1/7/2005	rich people plundering jobs,middle class (Jesus)	2/17/2005
possessions left on way to refuge (Jesus)	2/7/2005	riches & power becoming idols (Jesus)	2/11/2005
possessions vs. heaven choices in this life (Jesus)	2/19/2005	rising from the dead meaning explained (Jesus)	3/28/2005
power outages and fuel supply (Jesus)	3/10/2005	rosary & scapular Blessed Mother intercedes (Jesus)	3/17/2005
power outages have preparations (Jesus)	3/2/2005	sacrifice of Mass renewal of Jesus' death (Jesus)	1/18/2005
power outages keep extra food, fuel (Jesus)	1/20/2005	sacrilege receiving Eucharist in mortal sin (Jesus)	3/24/2005
prayer many needs for (Jesus)	3/10/2005	saints models of life (Jesus)	1/6/2005
prayer way to lighten burdens (Jesus)	1/13/2005	saints models to follow in life (Jesus)	1/20/2005
prayer for peace lessen disasters, change lives (Jesus)	2/12/2005	salvation Jesus died for love of all (Jesus)	1/4/2005
prayer groups chance to share faith (Jesus)	2/1/2005	saving souls most important duty (Jesus)	2/6/2005
prayer groups for spiritual support (Jesus)	3/2/2005	Schiavo, Terry euthanasia,quality of life (Jesus)	3/31/2005
prayer life communication with God (Jesus)	1/30/2005	sexual sins require life change to God (Jesus)	1/26/2005
prayer time priorities needed (Jesus)	2/18/2005	shame for sin do not forget (Jesus)	2/3/2005
prayer warriors holding back total destruction (Jesus)	1/12/2005	shelters like pagodas at refuges (Jesus)	2/3/2005
Precious Blood washes our sins (Jesus)	3/23/2005	shelters multiplied at refuges (Jesus)	2/3/2005
priests need prayers to keep holy (Jesus)	2/17/2005	Shroud of Turin caused by Resurrection (Jesus)	3/13/2005
priests pray for (Jesus)	3/10/2005	sick & disabled need your help (Jesus)	3/11/2005
priorities for a simple life (Jesus)	3/16/2005	simple life needed to avoid desire of wealth (Jesus)	1/18/2005
priorities of love & help others (Jesus)	3/3/2005	simpler life needed stop rushing (Jesus)	2/14/2005
prisoners need hope in the Spirit (Jesus)	1/13/2005	sin, everyone's Jesus took on (Jesus)	3/27/2005
prophets, messengers sent for each age, people (Jesus)	3/29/2005	sinful habits avoid occasions of sin (Jesus)	1/3/2005
public witness to faith will risk your life (Jesus)	1/29/2005	sinful lifestyle please God instead of self (Jesus)	1/26/2005
purgatory pray for souls there (Jesus)	3/17/2005	sinners seek forgiveness (Jesus)	3/10/2005
railroads carry dangerous chemicals (Jesus)	1/19/2005	sins strike Jesus (Jesus)	3/22/2005
Real Presence found in Eucharist (Jesus)	2/25/2005	sins flaunted have war & disasters (Jesus)	1/9/2005
refuge escape will need bicycles (Jesus)	2/3/2005	sins of America calling down God's wrath (Jesus)	1/12/2005
refuge, North Hills, Ca. shelter for many people (Jesus)	2/8/2005	smart cards becoming mandatory (Jesus)	2/10/2005
refuges deer meat provided (Jesus)	3/7/2005	snow uniqueness of flakes like us (Jesus)	1/7/2005
refuges have miracles of protection (Jesus)	3/2/2005	society lost sense of sin (Jesus)	1/9/2005
refuges leave possessions behind (Jesus)	1/7/2005	Sodom & Gomorrah like United States (Jesus)	3/12/2005
refuges modern day Exodus (Jesus)	2/27/2005	souls responsibility to save (Jesus)	1/17/2005
refuges place of protection (Jesus)	3/10/2005	souls drifting from God to worldly things (Jesus)	1/16/2005
refuges rustic setting in wilderness (Jesus)	2/7/2005	souls need saving be persistent in pursuing (Jesus)	1/28/2005
refuges shelters multiplied upwards (Jesus)	2/3/2005	sower,parable of Word of God in seed (Jesus)	1/23/2005
refuges shelters to be multiplied (Jesus)	2/3/2005	spiritual freedom glorifying God than self (Jesus)	1/13/2005
refuges signs to go to (Jesus)	3/14/2005	spiritual laziness blessings removed (Jesus)	3/9/2005
refuges give protection from disasters & diseases (Jesus)	2/12/2005	spiritual life need healing in conversion (Jesus)	2/13/2005
relatives in purgatory need prayers (Jesus)	2/16/2005	spiritual reading help toward perfection (Jesus)	2/8/2005
repent of sins to reconcile with God (Jesus)	2/26/2005	spiritual survival avoid deadly mortal sin (Jesus)	1/21/2005
Resurrection a foreshadowing for us (Jesus)	3/13/2005	spiritual umbrella in sacraments (Jesus)	2/22/2005
Resurrection hope for us too (Jesus)	3/17/2005	St. Joseph,Blessed Mother united wills (Jesus)	3/19/2005
Resurrection is hope for us too (Jesus)	3/20/2005	St. Patrick pray for his intercession (Jesus)	3/17/2005

Volume XXXVIII

standard of living lower because of exported jobs (Jesus)	1/27/2005
Stations of Cross on Fridays of Lent (Jesus)	2/17/2005
Stations of the Cross follow Jesus' footsteps (Jesus)	2/10/2005
statues, rosaries shared with prayer group (Jesus)	2/17/2005
stripping churches removes reverence,traditions (Jesus)	2/3/2005
suffering & penances ways to atone for sins (Jesus)	1/31/2005
taxes causing burdens (Jesus)	3/10/2005
teaching materials for tsunami victims (Jesus)	1/20/2005
terrorism because of hate of America (Jesus)	1/19/2005
time & talents share with others (Jesus)	1/3/2005
time for prayer tithing 10% of your time (Jesus)	1/30/2005
time, faith share with others (Jesus)	2/23/2005
time, wasting avoid worldly distractions (Jesus)	2/8/2005
Transfiguration glorified body (Jesus)	3/13/2005
treasure where your heart is (Jesus)	2/23/2005
treasures in heaven best to have at death (Jesus)	2/10/2005
tribulation faith will be tried (Jesus)	3/15/2005
tribulation need spiritual strength (Jesus)	3/2/2005
tribulation saved only by Jesus (Jesus)	2/27/2005
tribulation signs with increasing earthquakes (Jesus)	3/29/2005
Trinity shown at Jesus' Baptism (Jesus)	1/9/2005
trust in God overcomes fear (Jesus)	1/5/2005
tsunami & disaster show power of nature (Jesus)	1/4/2005
tsunami areas prostitution,porn & children (Jesus)	1/10/2005
tsunami disaster give help to them (Jesus)	1/6/2005
tsunami victims help generously (Jesus)	1/8/2005
underground church in future persecution (Jesus)	1/31/2005
underground cities secret for dignitaries (Jesus)	2/15/2005
underground shuttles connect secret cities (Jesus)	2/15/2005
volcanoes & earthquakes shake earth's core (Jesus)	3/5/2005
Warning a comet on day of (Jesus)	3/18/2005
Warning know not to take mark (Jesus)	3/12/2005
Warning only signs given, no dates (Jesus)	2/3/2005
Warning prepare with Confession (Jesus)	3/17/2005
Warning experience described (Jesus)	1/6/2005
Warning experience more back to Mass (Jesus)	2/20/2005
Warning to Jesus' return Transfiguration to Easter (Jesus)	2/20/2005
wars make peace instead (Jesus)	1/1/2005
wars oil & weapons needed (Jesus)	3/19/2005
wars pray for peace instead of (Jesus)	3/10/2005
wars & deficits promoted by the rich (Jesus)	2/15/2005
wars need stopping for peace, less deficits (Jesus)	2/3/2005
wars need to stop tell Congress to stop (Jesus)	1/29/2005
wars, constant speak out against war (Jesus)	1/20/2005
water chastisements for violating God's laws (Jesus)	1/16/2005
wealth share with others (Jesus)	3/3/2005
wealth, sharing gains merits in heaven (Jesus)	1/24/2005
weather chastisements of (Jesus)	3/10/2005
weather unusual storms as signs (Jesus)	1/11/2005
Yellowstone disasterous volcano (Jesus)	3/5/2005

More Messages

If you would like to take advantage of more precious words from Jesus and Mary and apply them to your lives, read the first three volumes of messages and visions given to us through John's special gift. Each book contains a full year of daily messages and visions. As Jesus and Mary said in volume IV:
Listen to My words of warning, and you will be ready to share in the beauty of the Second Coming. Jesus 7/4/96
I will work miracles of conversion on those who read these books with an open mind. Jesus 9/5/96

Prepare for the Great Tribulation and the Era of Peace

Volume I - *July 1993 to June 1994*, ISBN# 1-882972-69-4, 256pp.	$7.95
Volume II - *July 1994 to June 1995*, ISBN# 1-882972-72-4, 352pp.	$8.95
Volume III - *July 1995 to July 10, 1996*, ISBN# 1-882972-77-5, 384pp.	$8.95
Volume IV - *July 11, 1996 to Sept. 30, 1996*, ISBN# 1-882972-91-0, 104pp.	$3.95
Volume V - *Oct. 1, 1996 to Dec. 31, 1996*, ISBN# 1-882972-97-X, 120pp.	$3.95
Volume VI - *Jan. 1, 1997 to Mar. 31, 1997*, ISBN# 1-57918-002-7, 112pp.	$3.95
Volume VII - *April 1, 1997 to June 30, 1997*, ISBN# 1-57918-010-8, 112pp.	$3.95
Volume VIII - *July 1, 1997 to Sept. 30, 1997*, ISBN# 1-57918-053-1, 128pp.	$3.95
Volume IX - *Oct. 1, 1997 to Dec. 31, 1997*, ISBN# 1-57918-066-3, 168pp.	$3.95
Volume X - *Jan. 1, 1998 to Mar. 31, 1998*, ISBN# 1-57918-073-6, 116pp.	$3.95
Volume XI - *Apr. 1, 1998 to June 30, 1998*, ISBN# 1-57918-096-5, 128pp.	$3.95
Volume XII - *July 1, 1998 to Sept. 30, 1998*, ISBN# 1-57918-105-8, 128pp.	$3.95
Volume XIII - *Oct. 1, 1998 to Dec. 31, 1998*, ISBN# 1-57918-113-9, 134pp.	$3.95
Volume XIV - *Jan. 1, 1999 to Mar. 31, 1999*, ISBN# 1-57918-115-5, 128pp.	$3.95
Volume XV - *Apr. 1, 1999 to June 30, 1999*, ISBN# 1-57918-122-8, 128pp.	$3.95
Volume XVI - *July 1, 1999 to Sept. 31, 1999*, ISBN# 1-57918-126-0, 136pp.	$3.95
Volume XVII - *Oct. 1, 1999 to Dec. 31, 1999*, ISBN# 1-57918-156-2, 136pp.	$3.95
Volume XVII - *Jan. 1, 2000 to Mar. 31, 2000*, ISBN# 1-57918-158-9, 136pp.	$3.95
Volume XIX - *Apr. 1, 2000 to June 30, 2000*, ISBN# 1-57918-160-0, 136pp.	$3.95
Volume XX - *July 1, 2000 to Sept. 30, 2000*, ISBN# 1-57918-162-7, 136pp.	$3.95
Volume XXI - *Oct. 1, 2000 to Dec. 31, 2000*, ISBN# 1-57918-160-0, 136pp.	$3.95
Volume XXII - *Jan. 1, 2001 to Mar. 31, 2001*, ISBN# 1-57918-172-4, 136pp.	$3.95
Volume XXIII - *Apr. 1, 2001 to June 30, 2001*, ISBN# 1-57918-173-2, 136pp.	$3.95
Volume XXIV - *July 1, 2001 to Sept. 30, 2001*, ISBN# 1-57918-174-0, 136pp.	$3.95
Volume XXV - *Oct. 1, 2001 to Dec. 31, 2001*, ISBN# 1-57918-193-7, 136pp.	$3.95
Volume XXVI - *Jan. 1, 2002 to Mar. 31, 2002*, ISBN# 1-57918-198-1, 136pp.	$3.95
Volume XXVII - *Apr. 1, 2002 to June. 30, 2002*, ISBN# 1-57918-200-3, 136pp.	$3.95
Volume XXVIII - *July. 1, 2002 to Sept. 30, 2002*, ISBN# 1-57918-221-6, 136pp.	$3.95
Volume XXIX - *Oct. 1, 2002 to Dec. 31, 2002*, ISBN# 1-57918-231-3, 136pp.	$3.95
Volume XXX - *Jan. 1, 2003 to Mar. 31, 2003*, ISBN# 1-57918-235-6, 136pp.	$3.95
Volume XXXI - *Apr. 1, 2003 to June. 30, 2003*, ISBN# 1-57918-240-2, 136pp.	$3.95
Volume XXXII - *July. 1, 2003 to Sept. 30, 2003*, ISBN# 1-57918-245-3, 136pp.	$3.95
Volume XXXIII - *Oct. 1, 2003 to Dec. 31, 2003*, ISBN# 1-57918-248-8, 136pp.	$3.95
Volume XXXIV - *Jan. 1, 2004 to Mar. 31, 2004*, ISBN# 1-57918-263-1, 144pp.	$3.95
Volume XXXV - *Apr. 1, 2004 to June. 30, 2004*, ISBN# 1-57918-267-4, 136pp.	$3.95
Volume XXXVI - *July. 1, 2004 to Sept. 30, 2004*, ISBN# 1-57918-270-4, 144pp.	$4.95
Volume XXXVII - *Oct. 1, 2004 to Dec. 31, 2004*, ISBN# 1-57918-247-7, 144pp.	$4.95
Volume XXXVIII - *Jan. 1, 2005 to Mar. 31, 2005*, ISBN# 1-57918-276-3, 136pp.	$4.95